Face to Face

Peter Honey is a freelance management consultant and coauthor of *Developing Interactive Skills.*

Business Communication for Results

Peter Honey

A SPECTRUM BOOK

Prentice-Hall, Inc., Englewood Cliffs, N.J. 07632

Library of Congress Cataloging in Publication Data

HONEY, PETER.
  Face to face.

  (A Spectrum Book)
    1. Interpersonal relations. 2. Interpersonal
relations—Case studies. I. Title.
HM132.H64–1978   301.14   78-750
ISBN 0-13-298620-5
ISBN 0-13-298612-4 pbk.

First published 1976 by Institute of Personnel Management,
London, England. © 1976 by P. Honey.
First American edition © 1978
by Prentice-Hall, Inc., Englewood Cliffs, N.J. 07632

A SPECTRUM BOOK

Printed in the United States of America

10 9 8 7 6 5 4 3 2 1

PRENTICE-HALL INTERNATIONAL, INC., *London*
PRENTICE-HALL OF AUSTRALIA PTY., LIMITED, *Sydney*
PRENTICE-HALL OF CANADA, LTD., *Toronto*
PRENTICE-HALL OF INDIA PRIVATE, LIMITED, *New Delhi*
PRENTICE-HALL OF JAPAN, INC., *Tokyo*
PRENTICE-HALL OF SOUTHEAST ASIA PTE., LTD., *Singapore*
WHITEHALL BOOKS, LIMITED, *Wellington, New Zealand*

To Carol, my wife, for more than usual forbearance in the face of interactive skills. To Mary Peddie for typing it all and correcting the spelling. To the hundreds and hundreds of managers I have worked with on various interactive skill ventures, all of whom have helped me to learn.

Contents

Preface

This book is about behavior in face to face encounters or interactions. It argues that behavior is critical in human relationships precisely because it is the part of us that is readily evident to other people. Their attitudes toward us and, more importantly, their *behavior* toward us are largely determined by our behavior toward them. This interaction between people's behavior is important because it in large part affects what is achieved or not achieved. This means that each of us has behavioral responsibilities and interactive skills are, in essence, about meeting those responsibilities through being thoughtful and thus consciously employing certain behaviors in certain situations.

In many ways the interactive skills approach, in common with other approaches that seek to help people to modify their behavior, places unpalatable demands on us. It demands specificity rather than ambiguity, discipline rather than disorder, conscious control rather than spontaneity. It also assumes that interactive skills, unrelieved by gimmicks or golden rules, have to be learned and worked at continuously lest we fall into unthinking modes of behavior. Initially, this may seem an unnatural struggle but, as with the acquisition of *any* skill, with practice the skills become absorbed as an unobtrusive part of us. When you are learning to ride a bicycle it is faster to walk: When you are learning to think about behavior it is easier not to!

Any approach that acknowledges the influence of behavior is bound to arouse ethical concerns. For the most part, these concerns are healthy and help to safeguard us against manipulative practices. Often, however, these concerns lead to an ostrich-like refusal to recognize behavior as an influential factor at all or to the absurd claim that all that matters is that your behavior should be an accurate reflection of your underlying feelings. Is it unethical to admit to trying to control behavior so that it is appropriate to the circumstances of a situation? It depends when and how it is done, of course, and this is precisely the line taken by an interactive skills approach: that there is a time and a place for every behavior and that the crucial skill is deciding when and where. This book unashamedly encourages you to practice the skills involved in arranging your behavior so that it is "in step" with objectives and the circumstances of the situation. It does so believing that we desperately need to learn to interact more competently in all our encounters, whether at work or at home.

Interactive skills and similar approaches are frequently criticized as being manipulative. Naturally, this is taken up at intervals throughout the text; but suffice at this stage to say that manipulation is about being furtive, clandestine, and ambiguous.

Interactive skills, on the other hand, are about being open and explicit. Objectives, for example, cannot be shared between people unless they are in a form capable of articulation. Similarly, things cannot be fruitfully agreed, or disagreed for that matter, unless specific communication skills are employed; trust cannot grow unless there is sufficient match between what is said and what is done, and so on. Interactive skills, like any other skills, are amoral. They can be used for the forces of good or for the forces of evil. You can use your skills to sell a good product or an inadequate one, to persuade people to a proper or improper course of action, to help people subscribe to mutually advantageous objectives or to trick them into subscribing to selfish one-sided ones. One of the best safeguards against the misuse of interactive skills is to have as many people as possible actively employing the five basic skills described later. The more skillful and behaviorally competent we are, the less likely it is that we shall fall prey to manipulative practices, either as consumers or as providers.

Throughout the book I have deliberately avoided referring to other behavioral approaches. This is because the book sets out to be a *practical* guide, an empirical rather than an erudite text. Should this make you feel isolated and starved of "proof statements," as sales parlance would have it, may I reassure you that the interactive skills approach described in the chapters which follow closely parallels and, indeed, *complements* other apparently "rival" approaches. The behavioral techniques typical of interactive skills can enhance other approaches of which I, at the time of writing, am aware. Let me cite a couple to show how I think this is possible.

First, the Managerial Grid (for an introductory text, read the book of that name by Blake and Mouton, 1964, Gulf Publishing Company) which, in summary, was developed from the simple premise that managerial styles emerge from the way a manager resolves the conflict, or dilemma, between concern for production on the one hand and concern for people on the other. Blake plots these concerns on a "grid" and pinpoints five "pure" styles and acknowledges the presence of many more permutations. The five are: high concern for production with low concern for people; low concern for production coupled with high concern for people; low concern for both; high concern for both; and, finally, a compromise position with moderate concern for both. From these basic positions on the Grid, Blake is able to pinpoint predominant behavior styles, since each Grid position predisposes a manager to behave in certain characteristic ways when it comes to decision-making, conflict resolution, expression of attitudes and emotion, use of humor, and the investment of effort.

Secondly, Transactional Analysis (for an introductory text, |read *I'm OK—You're OK* by Harris, 1973, Harper and Row), recently developed into a commonsense approach to understanding your own and other people's behavior from the mystical depths of psychiatry. According to Transactional Analysis (TA), everyone has three typical modes of behavior. They are the Child ego state, or the "felt concept of life," which includes feelings of frustration, inadequacy, helplessness, joy, curiosity, spontaneity, and the like; the Parent ego state, or the "taught concept of life," which includes moralizing, being righteous or accusing, and generally laying down the law; and, finally, the Adult ego state, or the "thought concept of life," which is that part of us that thinks things out and makes decisions by collecting and looking at facts, estimating probabilities, and so on. These three modes of behavior are coupled to certain assumptions that TA claims we all make about ourselves in relation to other people. The assumptions are called life positions and can be classified into one of the following four categories: I'm Not OK and You're OK; I'm OK and You're Not OK; I'm Not OK and You're Not OK; and I'm OK and You're OK. In general, the approach which, like the Grid, has much more to it than is mentioned here, argues that we should develop our adult ego state and lock into the I'm OK and You're OK life position.

There are considerable similarities between the Grid, Transactional Analysis, and Interactive Skills. For example, they are all attempts to describe behavior in a meaningful, helpful way; and all assume that the behavior adopted makes a difference to the outcome. Also, all assume that being conscious of behavior is a necessary prerequisite before being able to modify or change it, and, interestingly, all three approaches put most energy into describing aspects of behavior that *can* change. A final and heartening similarity is that all three argue for increased openness, explicitness, and straightness between people. Transactional Analysis does this by being keen on "authenticity," the Grid favors "candor," and Interactive Skills include such goings-on as labeling behavior, *saying* objectives, planning rather than intending, and so on. Perhaps the most significant overlap is between the five basic interactive skills and what in Transactional Analysis is called "Adult." When TA suggests you use your Adult ego state, it is in effect inviting you consciously to use the five basic skills of diagnosing the situation, setting appropriate objectives, arranging "in step" behaviors, controlling behavior accordingly, and monitoring your own and other people's behavior. In other words, being "Adult" exactly matches what in this book we term interactive skills.

There are, though, differences between the three approaches. For one thing, the descriptive level varies. TA is very general, encompassing the whole of life; the Grid concentrates on management styles; and the interactive skills approach confines itself to behavior in fact to face interactions. Another significant difference is the relative weight the approaches give to matters like attitudes which lurk beneath the surface of behavior itself. Both the Grid and TA assume that it is necessary to understand underlying attitudes because they are the stuff of which behavior is made. The interactive skills approach, on the other hand, is more ruthlessly behavioral, putting relatively less emphasis on attitudes and arguing that underlying attitudes need not necessarily dictate, or cause, the overt display of behavior itself. Clearly this is an awful dilemma which runs right through the behavioral sciences: whether to change behavior and let attitudes look after themselves, or whether to change attitudes and let behavior fall in line accordingly. The interactive skills approach is convinced that for all practical purposes—and remember, this is a practical guide to interactive skills—it is behavior itself that matters in face to face interaction, and that much can be done to modify and extend it irrespective of underlying attitudes.

A final difference between the approaches, and this is where the interactive skills approach seems to succeed in *enhancing* both the Grid and Transactional Analysis, is in how far they accompany you along the road to behavior change. The Grid and TA drop you off earlier than interactive skills because they aim more at increasing *awareness* about behavioral issues than on *how* to change. Interactive skills, as you will quickly find, is much more to do with the mechanics of changing your own and other people's behavior and regards awareness as a useful prerequisite but not a sufficient condition for change. This difference tends to loop us back to the points just made about attitudes and behavior. Clearly, if your priority is to change attitudes, you keep hammering away at awareness. If your priority is to change behavior, then you need a behavior therapist's techniques, including a precise *plan* for change, reinforcement, and feedback. I therefore believe that the interactive skills described in this book are the means of accepting, should you wish to, the Grid's invitation to overhaul your managerial style, TA's invitation to become more Adult and adopt the I'm OK—You're OK stance, and the behavioral science's invitation to become learning rather than learned in our people dealings.

Peter Honey

1

Introducing
Behavior

The main emphasis throughout this book is on the practice, rather than the theory, of interactive skills. You may feel that the very expression "interactive skills" belies this claim immediately, but I hope to make you easily and quickly familiar with a few pieces of what you could call jargon.

Initially, we can say that interactive skills are the skills you or I use in face to face encounters to arrange our behavior so that it is in step with our objectives. This means that interactive skills have very little to do with being nice or winning friends, unless those sorts of outcomes are encapsulated in the objectives. The whole idea is to see how successful we can be at using our behavior to increase the probability of achieving our objectives. Our behavior is a means that can, depending on our skill, either help or hinder us in achieving our ends.

Before we explore the various techniques in subsequent chapters, it is important to agree on a few basics. I have already used the word behavior, for example, so what does that actually refer to? Even more fundamental is the whole issue of whether behavior matters anyway. Does the way we behave during an interaction really make a significant difference to the outcome? Even if it does, where does it come in the roster of influential factors? Is it just an "optional extra," or is our behavior an essential ingredient? Does it *always* matter, or are there interactive situations where it is appropriate to "freewheel" and not consciously concern ourselves with behavioral issues?

These and questions like them are the primary concern of this first chapter.

BEHAVIOR DEFINED

First, what do I mean by behavior? The word is not exactly a piece of jargon, but that is precisely its danger. At least if a word strikes us as jargon it is likely to provoke a query as to its meaning. The word behavior is one with which we are all familiar. Indeed, most people associate it particularly with childhood where warnings about the need to behave properly were prevalent!

"Behavior" refers, quite simply, to everything we do which is overt or observable. It therefore embraces an enormous range: reflexes, like our leg jerking when the muscles are hit in a certain position or like the pupils of our eyes contracting and expanding under different light conditions; all sorts of learned habits, like riding a bicycle, tying shoe laces, nodding approval when people say something we agree with—the whole gamut of verbal and nonverbal actions and reactions of which we are capable.

The range is so great that I shall cream off the behavior we use in interactive situations for primary attention in this book. Accordingly, we shall not be paying attention to muscular reflexes or to what are known as "motor" habits (walking, swimming, driving a car, etc.), because they are not very significant in face to face interactions between people. Our concern is with what are variously called interpersonal, social, or communicating behavior: the words we speak to make our point; the intonation we use; the accompanying nonverbal behavior like facial expressions, gestures with our hands, and the bodily posture we adopt (referred to, quite literally, by many researchers as our body *language*).

The main point to grasp is that behavior is *always* directly observable. This may seem a trite point to be starting with, but the implications are considerable. For example, I shall argue that one of the reasons our behavior is important is precisely because it is so immediately visible to others. The people we interact with can *see* our facial expressions and they can *hear* our words. The conclusions they reach about us are primarily based on this visible behavior. The conclusions we reach about them are based, quite naturally, on our observations of their behavior. In a sense, our behavior is all we have got going for us in our face to face dealings with people.

A further implication which we shall explore in much more detail is that because our behavior quite literally "shows" it has a direct impact on the behavior we get back from other people. I shall illustrate later how behavior is infectious (you yawn, they yawn; you smile, they smile, and so on). I shall also show how it is possible to influence the reactions of others by using your own behavior to "shape" theirs.

DISTINCTION BETWEEN BEHAVIOR, ATTITUDES, EMOTIONS, AND OTHER UNDERLYING FACTORS

If we define behavior as all we do that is overt, doesn't that leave a lot unsaid? Is this too superficial a definition? What about important things like attitudes, feelings, and motives? Surely our behavior, when all is said and done, is only the tip of an iceberg?

I am not suggesting that our behavior is *all* there is to us, merely that it is the most *visible* aspect—just like the tip of an iceberg, in fact. Beneath our behavioral surface lurk all sorts of enormously complicated underlying factors, so complicated that behavioral scientists are nowhere near to unraveling all the variables and explaining why people behave as they do. In broad terms, our behavior is the visible output resulting from the interpretations we make about the world about us. We are always operating within an external environment of some kind, and our senses are continually at work absorbing information about our surroundings. There is too much for us consciously to pay attention to everything and so we operate a number of filters. We pay close attention to, say, the people in our meeting, keep half an eye on the clock on the wall, and pay no attention to the distant noise of passing traffic. As soon as something fairly dramatic happens, we switch our attention, if only momentarily, to that: A plane flies over, a secretary arrives with coffee, the room gets too hot, and so on.

All this information goes, via our senses, into a sort of central processor where it is sorted, interpreted, and given meaning. This is a remarkable process which is unique to each person. It seems that our past experience in sifting all the incoming information leaves a residue of learning. The conclusions we have reached in the past contaminate, to a greater or lesser extent, our future interpretations. If we concluded that so and so was a fuddy duddy last time we had dealings with him, it will certainly predispose us to view him in that light again. Our attitude towards him is important because, unless we deliberately control our behavior, it will affect the overt reactions we display towards him. That may or may not matter, of course, depending on our relationship with him and on our purposes for the interaction with him.

The residue we accrue from handling millions of pieces of information in our central processor combines together to result in our capabilities (what we can do and can't do) on the one hand, and our inclinations (what we want to do and don't want to do) on the other. The knowledge and skills we acquire through formal and informal learning are two important factors that play a part in determining our capabilities, for example. On the other hand, our attitudes, feelings, temperament, moods, and our motives and interests are examples of the sorts of factors that influence our inclinations.

I shall not dwell on these underlying factors to any great extent because, important though they are in helping us to understand the totality of our personal make-up, they are not primarily what this book is about. We are concerned with the skills involved in arranging manifest behavior so that it is appropriate to objectives and the circumstances of the situations in which we find ourselves. The emphasis is therefore, quite properly, going to be on behavior itself: on what goes on between people above the behavioral surface.

Largely to disregard the interplay between underlying factors such as knowledge, skills, attitudes, and emotions is not as superficial as it might at first appear. There is plenty of evidence to suggest that these sorts of beneath the surface factors do not enjoy a monopoly in determining why people behave as they do. Why is it, for example, that if you smile at people, not inanely but nevertheless fairly frequently, it has the effect of "causing" them to increase their smiling rate significantly? Why is it, to use another simple nonverbal example, that if you nod your head while people are talking to you it "causes" them to talk for longer than if you keep your head still?

These examples serve to remind us that our behavior, visible and manifest, often has a fairly direct influence on the behavior of others or vice versa. It is true that *all* observations of behavior go through the central processor before an output, such as a return reaction, appears. But the point is that much behavior can be satisfactorily explained at a behavioral level; and it is not always necessary for us to have recourse to underlying factors either to understand behavior or to change it.

The advantage of this emphasis on visible behavior itself is that we do not need to become amateur, or even professional, psychologists before we can be successful in our interactions with people as managers, salesmen, politicians, or personnel specialists. We *do* need to become good at basic skills such as observing behavior accurately, arranging our own behavior appropriately, and controlling our behavior accordingly. It is these basic skills that this book is about.

When I advance these arguments, people often ask: "But surely we must take people's attitudes and feelings into account when we interact with them?" My answer is that of course it is important to have emphathy for the feelings of others. In doing so, we must recognize that inferring the presence or absence of certain motives, feelings, and attitudes in others will always have to be speculative. This is because the underlying factors are invisible. You cannot have direct access to the attitudes of others, nor to their emotions, nor, for that matter, to their skills, knowledge, and intelligence.

The best you can do is to observe their behavior and, working backwards from that, "guess" about the presence or absence of these things. Once again, we see that behavior itself is different in kind from the underlying factors. Behavior is visible; underlying factors are invisible.

Behavior emerges again as an attribute of special importance. You may like someone very much and find them a pleasure to do business with; but, unless you behave as if you do, they will never know. Conversely, you may be utterly bored by your interactions with someone and wish that they wouldn't be so long-winded; but unless you "behave it" they cannot know. In a very real sense, this is why the behavioral sciences tend to emphasize the importance of openness, explicitness, and candor between people. It stems from the realization that relationships depend on how people behave in the face to face dealings they have with one another. Extremely shy or introverted people are handicapped in the sense that they frequently fail to generate enough explicit behavior. The tend to "sell other people short" behaviorally and therefore to leave them uncomfortable about the interaction. How often have you been left guessing about whether so and so was quiet because he agreed with everything and was therefore content to acquiesce silently? Or because he was bored and not listening? Or because he disapproved but didn't like to say so? Your interpretations have to be based on the behavior you observed. If you are left short of behavior then the more you are left guessing.

Many practices that we take for granted stem from this basic distinction between behavior itself and underlying factors. For example, because it is not possible to know what someone *feels* about his work, ways and means have been devised to get people to *say* what they feel. Attitude surveys, questionnaires, and interviews all have this basic aim. Once someone has been encouraged to articulate his feelings, some behavior has been provoked that can be listened to, absorbed, probed further, and so on. Examinations were invented with similar basic aims. Since it is not possible to know whether someone knows something or not, he or she has to be stimulated into overtly demonstrating whether they knew it by, for example, answering an examination question or, in practical exams, by physically demonstrating that they possess the knowledge (and, perhaps skills). People who are not able to behave well in examination conditions suffer badly because judgments about the extent of their knowledge are indirectly based on the overt behavior itself. Once again, behavior is shown to be a crucial factor. At best, you can only guess about other people's underlying factors. Their behavior you can be quite certain about.

BEHAVIOR AND PERSONALITY

Perhaps it would be helpful to clear up another basic confusion that worries people when highlighting the distinction between behavior and other associated variables. The query that often comes up is about the relationship between personality and behavior. Are they the same? If not, what is the difference, and is it of any importance?

Using an analogy seems the simplest way in which to draw the distinction between personality and behavior.

Imagine you are a goat in a field. You are tethered by a rope to a stake that has been driven into the ground and is made fast. The position of the stake in the field and the length of the rope quite naturally determines the area you can roam. Strain as you might, they set limits on your freedom. There are parts of the field you cannot get to. On the other hand, providing your tether is not cruelly short, you have plenty of room to maneuver with the stake as a central point. Let us call the circumference around the stake your personality. In other words, your personality sets boundaries beyond which you can't go. No one is quite agreed on a totally satisfactory definition of personality, but there is a consensus that it is a global term summing up all the ingredients that we have already mentioned as capabilities and inclinations. Your personality is, if you like, the thread of consistency that runs through everything you do. The consistencies are considerable, even though it is popular to claim that people are largely unpredictable. When you claim to *know* someone well, for example, what that actually means is that you have sampled their behavior sufficiently to say that you feel fairly confident about predicting how they will behave in the future. Even inconsistent people are consistently inconsistent!

So personality is an umbrella term summing up our totality. Part of us, as we have already seen, can be singled out for special attention and called our behavior. The relationship between the two is now clear. Personality sets the constraints or boundaries, but within it we are able to behave in various ways and even, if we wish, to make considerable modifications to our behavior. Personality, by the time we are adults—and probably much earlier—is relatively fixed and unchanging. Our overt behavior, however, is amenable to a process of continual modification and change. Personality can change when something really dramatic intervenes: the equivalent of pulling up the goat's stake and driving it into the ground in another field altogether. Brainwashing, certain drugs, and brain damage can alter the threads of consistency running through someone's behavior. Short of such drastic happenings, we are free within the confines set by our personalities to experiment with our behavior.

Most people do not do so, however. In fact, researchers show time and time again that most of us are stuck in well-worn behavioral ruts. Even though we may *claim* to adapt our behavior to changing circumstances, people, and situations that we encounter, most of us fail to use anything like the full range of behavioral options that our personalities leave open to us.

It is rather like the goat always grazing close to the stake and never moving out to the extremities, or like the goat only grazing, say, a 90° segment and leaving the other three quarters unexplored.

One of the hallmarks of an interactively skilled person is that he or she has a behavioral repertoire which is wide enough to give them genuine choice in deciding how best to behave in differing situations. Sometimes they hog it and do most of the talking. At other times they sit back and listen. Sometimes they produce lots of ideas. At others they hold back their own ideas and tease suggestions out of other people. Sometimes they choose to behave with absolute certainty, at other times to behave hesitantly, and so on.

DOES BEHAVIOR MATTER?

So far, I hope to have shown you that behavior is always overt and therefore directly observable and that, unless they are directly translated into behavior, underlying attitudes, emotions, and so on are invisible. We have also looked at the relationship between overt behavior and the total compass of personality itself. That leaves the question: Does the way we behave in face to face interactions with people actually matter? To what extent is behavior an influential factor in determining the outcome of our interactions?

Insofar as we have already established that people's judgments about us stem from their observations of our behavior, it would seem to be clear that our behavior matters very much.

Certainly whenever we are in situations where we wish to impress or to gain personal credibility, our behavior is absolutely crucial in determining whether we shall succeed or not. Take, for example, the situation that a personnel manager is in: He usually has limited executive authority to wield when cajoling line management into behaving responsibly with the human resources at the organization's disposal. More often, he has to fall back on his skills of persuasion. As every wise personnel manager knows, it is not solely the *quality* of the suggestions he puts forward, in terms of their logic, practicability, and so on that wins the day: Certainly his personal credibility with the line is equally important. If the line management's observations of his previous behavior has led it to have a low regard for him and the contribution he can make, even if he then comes up with a first class idea it is unlikely to be heeded.

Some people think that when personal credibility plays such a significant part in someone's success it is some sort of outrage and a rather cynical example of how gullible human beings are. Perhaps you believe that this emphasis on behavior is rather trite and missing the point? Certainly some people are irritated to learn that the effort they put into arguing logically is often completely negated by their inability to arrange their accompanying behavior appropriately.

This is not to suggest that our behavior is the sole or even the most important factor in determining our effectiveness. But it is *one* of the factors, and one that we can choose to harness to our advantage.

Let us take another example. The other day a salesman came to advise my wife on an efficient layout for her kitchen. He did not explicitly announce his objective, but let us suppose that it was to win an order that would result in the firm he represented installing its kitchen furniture and fittings. He went about this task in a way that led my wife to conclude it was all rather a bore: just routine, that he'd done hundreds like it before. He asked relatively few questions.

He grumbled a bit about some of the odd shapes in the kitchen, explaining what a problem they were if all the space were to be fully used. He showed her pamphlets and sample working surfaces in rather a diffident take it or leave it way. He left promising to submit drawings and a full quotation for the work. The next day a salesman representing a competitive company came for his appointment. He was late, as it happened, but he had telephoned to say so and to apologize in advance. As soon as he saw the kitchen, he made complimentary comments. He didn't overdo it, but left my wife with the impression that the kitchen with its odd shapes and angles had caught his interest. He asked my wife lots of questions about her needs and paid careful attention to her ideas. He actively supported many of them, developed others, and suggested some alternatives, explaining their advantages. He had a squared sheet of paper in his briefcase that he used to draw a plan of the kitchen, and then he placed model kitchen cabinets, sink units and so on in different positions to test my wife's reactions to alternative layouts. He left promising to submit drawings and a full quotation for the work.

When the quotations came, they were remarkably similar. The cabinets they were proposing also looked much the same. The first salesman's use of one of the awkward corners was rather better than the other's. Despite this, there was no doubt that the second salesman had won the order. His behavior had been the deciding factor.

I know a president of a company who is enormously demanding in his behavior. He has a reputation for being a stickler over detail. He asks devastatingly perceptive questions and has an uncanny knack of uncovering weaknesses and areas where people's knowledge is shaky and uncertain. He always plays devil's advocate; he rarely accepts presentations, ideas, and proposals, first time around, and sends people scurrying back to dig out additional details. To cap it all, everything must always be done at once if not sooner. The effect that this behavior has on his direct subordinates, all vice-presidents, is predictable. They have learned to keep their heads down and have developed various strategies to protect themselves. They are naturally reluctant to make decisions, they delay and procrastinate, they cause things to be worked and reworked to excess. They are forced to pay pathological attention to detail and to work overlong hours.

This manager's behavior is of prime importance in affecting the working atmosphere and performance of his colleagues and, ultimately, via them, of the whole organization. It may be that this executive has thought about the consequences of behaving as he does. He may have decided that it is appropriate after taking stock of his directors and the state of the company. Be that as it may, my concern at the moment is to show, through examples, that behavior does make a significant difference to the behavior of others and therefore, in turn, to the results we achieve in face to face interaction.

I know a doctor in general practice who is the senior partner in a group of doctors. He is short of patients. He has plenty on his register, but they avoid actually seeing him because he treats his patients as if they are stupid. When they call for an appointment at the office they ask for the junior partner. Yet the junior partner actually knows less, professionally, than the senior doctor. It is the difference in behavior that accounts for the unpopularity of one and the high demand for the other. The same happens with clergy. Some have full churches, some have empty ones. The explanation is not always, but usually, to be found in the singer, not the song.

Quite clearly, behavior is not the only factor that determines the success of salesmen, managers, doctors, and clergy. A host of noninteractive skills play a part too: factors such as how hard they work, their technical or professional know-how, their temperament when it comes to making decisions, their basic stance toward people—whether, for example, they move away or toward other people. These and many more are all aspects of behavior that distinguish between people. They are also examples of behavior that does not necessarily play a large part in determining someone's *interactive* skills: the behavior he uses when he is in face to face interaction with other people.

Other factors are involved in determining someone's success. These are those that are *external* to the actual person under consideration. Our president's success, for example, does not just hinge on his behavioral characteristics—interactive and noninteractive—but also on factors like the size and performance of the company, the nature of its product, the competence of key people in the organization, the state of the market, competitors' activities, and the financial climate.

Here is one further example to show behavior in its proper perspective. The effectiveness of a personnel manager hinges not only on his interactive competence and personal credibility but also on other factors such as the enlightenment of members of line management as the consumers of personnel services, because they are so influential in shaping what those services shall be; the phase of development of the company, because there are differing pressures depending on whether it is in the "establishing itself/ entrepreneurial phase" or the "consolidating/bedding down phase" or the "slimming down for survival phase." Other examples include the funding of the personnel function; the trade unions, because their activities make a vast difference to what the personnel manager can spend his time on; and, not least, factors to do with the professional personnel expertise of the personnel manager and his subordinates and colleagues in the personnel function.

In summary, I hope to have shown at the outset that our behavior in face to face interaction with other people is one among several factors that helps to determine our success and effectiveness. Behavior, however, is a factor that many people choose to ignore or to acknowledge grudgingly. In part, this is because they have not understood how it is possible deliberately to arrange and control their behavior according to the circumstances in which they find themselves. There are also strong reservations about doing this. It is argued that to lay on a deliberate display of overt behavior that is not necessarily an accurate reflection of the underlying feelings and attitudes is in some sense dishonest. But having straight, open dealings with people does not necessarily mean that you *have* to reveal your underlying feelings in your overt behavior. Whether you do so or not depends on your analysis of the situation and the objectives you wish to achieve with the people with whom you are interacting.

There is another practical snag in allowing feelings to dictate behavior. If, for example, you are feeling displeased with your secretary because she has misplaced something, the feelings may spill over into your behavior in various ways. You could be rather brusque with her. You could criticize her work. You could suddenly return some of her typing when normally you accept it at that standard. You could actually say something like "I must admit I'm feeling a bit cross with you today because you lost that letter that I needed for yesterday's meeting." These are just four alternative ways in which your underlying feelings of annoyance might be reflected in your behavior. The first three are ambiguous. They leave the secretary largely in the dark about why you are being brusque, hypercritical, and returning her work when normally you would accept it. She cannot possibly *know* why because, remember, she only has access to your behavior and has to work backwards from what is observable to reach conclusions about underlying factors. This is how misunderstandings between people arise.

So even if you *are* going to allow your feelings to spill over into your overt behavior you still, in many circumstances, need consciously to arrange the behavior so that it achieves whatever you wish it to achieve without all sorts of unwanted consequences. Clearly, there are many situations where it would be inappropriate to allow your underlying feelings to dictate your behavior. In a delicate negotiation with the unions it can be cataclysmic to allow, say, feelings of frustration to burst out onto the behavioral surface. One of the joys of being interactively skillful is that you can deliberately engineer your overt behavior to give the desired impression and not be at the mercy of your subjective feelings.

There is a time and a place for subjective feelings, a time and a place for you to blow your top, and even a time and a place for relaxing behaviorally and not giving it conscious thought. Just when is it worth going to the trouble consciously to arrange and control behavior? The short answer to that is this: whenever you are in a situation where you are conscious of wanting to achieve something—of having some objectives, in fact—then it behooves you to arrange your overt behavior so that it facilitates the achievement of those objectives. Objectives, rather than feelings, dictate behavior. Whenever you have objectives to persuade or influence people or to impress them, your behavior is a critical factor in determining the outcome. When you are in prickly situations, where emotions are running high and one ill-considered word can be a turning point, your behavior is crucial. Whenever you are in a situation, where the people present have conflicting objectives, behavior is crucial in steering the interaction through to a fruitful conclusion.

On the other hand, on many interactive occasions we are not actively conscious of wishing to achieve an objective: when we relax at the bar with friends, for example, when we pass the time of day in inconsequential chitchat with people. I hesitate to say "at home" with our families because perhaps one of the reasons why there is often so much strife on the home front is because people reckon it is safe to "relax"; consequently, behavior is often abominable in all sorts of crucial family interactions when objectives go unheeded and behavior is not arranged accordingly. Few would seriously doubt that the way parents behave in their dealings with their children is enormously influential in their development, and the same applies to teachers. A fascinating experiment demonstrated just how powerful a factor the behavior of teachers is. Having tested the intelligence of vast numbers of children in different schools and towns, the experimenters leaked news back to certain teachers about the performance of certain children. Unbeknown to the teachers, the news was false. They would let it slip that so and so was a lad with a lot of potential when he had in fact put in a below average performance on the intelligence tests. The teachers were of course very surprised about this, so much so that they modified their behavior towards the pupils in question—small things like giving them more time, being more encouraging, and showing less exasperation. One year later, the whole experiment was repeated. Hundreds of children were rated for intelligence and the pupils about whom false news had been leaked back had all made bigger improvements, measured in an increase in IQ points, than was average for the sample. There were other variables at work, but clearly the teachers' behavior was the big factor in determining this change: another instance of the crucial influence of overt behavior.

SUMMARY

We defined interactive skills as those used in face to face encounters when arranging behavior so that it is in step with objectives. Behavior was also defined as everything we do, verbal and nonverbal, which is overt and therefore directly observable by others.

This definition was used to distinguish between behavior itself and underlying factors such as attitudes, motives, and feelings. We found that behavior is visible, and thus makes a more direct impact on the behavior of others. Attitudes are invisible and can only show themselves in behavior itself.

We moved on to explore the relationship between personality and behavior. Personality was found to be an all-embracing term setting overall limits on what we could do. The constraints imposed by our personalities, however, left plenty of room for behavioral adaptation.

One of the main objects of this chapter was to give examples to show that behavior is a factor that can make a considerable difference to our interactive performance. We saw how behavior is one factor among others that conspire together to determine our success or failure.

Finally, we argued that more attention would be paid to behavior as an influential factor if more people knew how to set about arranging and controlling it. We finished by identifying when it is worth troubling consciously to arrange behavior. The short answer was that it was worth doing so whenever we were in a face to face situation and consciously aware of wishing to achieve some objective.

2

Situations, Objectives, and Behavior

The remainder of this book has to be based on certain assumptions. This is because the behavioral area is relatively fraught with uncertainty and half truths. Opinions on many major issues still outweigh hard black and white facts in the behavioral sciences. This is why it is only fair to share explicitly the assumptions that underpin this book. I am admitting to some of my biases and prejudices at the outset so that you can compare them with yours and have early warning of any mismatch.

The first assumption is that the way we behave in face to face encounters with people *does* matter; that our behavior affects the behavior of others and therefore, in turn, the results we achieve. This assumption was explored in the last chapter to the extent that I hope you can join me in subscribing to it, at any rate, for the time being.

The second main assumption is that there is no single panacea-like correct behavior style. This is an inconvenient thing to believe. It would obviously simplify things greatly to have a well-proven behavioral approach that stands us in good stead in all situations, with all people, always. Unfortunately, behavioral rights and wrongs are more difficult to come by. Our experience should tell us that if the situations and the people we encounter vary, our behavioral approach should vary also. Sometimes the variations in approach need only be slight. Sometimes they will need to be considerable. The point is that the rights and wrongs of behavior only make sense in the light of situations, other people, and objectives. There is no panacea. This explains why, maddeningly, behavioral scientists always hedge their answers with expressions like "it all depends." One manager was recently relieved to learn that the appropriateness or inappropriateness of his behavior depended on the circumstances of the situation he was dealing with at the time. "At least," he said, "that means that by sheer chance I'm bound to be right *some of the time!*" In a sense he was right. There *is* a time and a place for most behaviors.

Thirdly, and this chapter is mainly concerned with developing this assumption, I am assuming that the maxim "If you have got objectives, your behavior should be in step with them" is not too sweeping a Great Truth. It will show how objectives can provide a meaningful backdrop against which to view behavior; and there will be some examples to demonstrate the usefulness of this in-step-out-of-step concept. This is a relatively easy way of making judgments about the appropriateness of your own as well as other people's behavior.

The fourth assumption is the most contentious. It is that on many occasions we need *consciously* to organize our behavior. In fact, this assumption tends to follow from the first three. If you subscribe to them, inevitably you must conclude that behavior needs to be consciously "arranged" to fit the bill on many occasions. Let us just check that: In summary, the first three assumptions were that behavior *does* matter; that there is no single correct behavior style; and that behavior should be "in step" with objectives. Is the need to plan, organize, and control behavior an inevitable consequence of these?

There are, certainly, staunch objectors to this last

assumption. Many people treasure the spontaneity of behavior above all else, arguing that it is "dishonest" deliberately to lay on a display of overt behavior that, for example, does not reflect underlying feelings accurately enough. Does this mean that we should allow our feelings to dictate our behavior? If so, all sorts of standards of behavior that have been built into our society are going to have to change. It means we could "blow our tops" just when we felt like it, irrespective of the consequences; we could break down and cry just when we felt like it; we could be silent and not speak to people just when we felt like it. Surely a much sounder basis is to let our objectives dictate our behavior? To do so helps us to understand that on some occasions it is entirely appropriate to allow our feelings to spill out into our overt behavior and that on others it is not. The objectives become the key, not feelings.

This leads one to conclude that it is rather more dishonest to conceal our *objectives* from people than it is to conceal our feelings. As I shall show later, one of the hallmarks of an interactively skilled person is that they frequently declare their objectives openly and explicitly. Even if they do not declare them, it should be easy for others to *work them out*. If the behavior is "in step" then the objectives will, to some extent, be transparent.

Another objection that people make to the notion that behavior should be organized and controlled is that to do so sets up internal stresses that are bad for you. They argue that the effort involved in consciously controlling behavior, instead of relaxing and letting it "rip," takes its toll over time and gives people breakdowns, ulcers, coronaries, and the like! But an enlightened person who has mastered the skills involved in consciously arranging behavior can do this without stress. *Learning* the skills is stressful, but this applies to the acquisition of any skill. When you are learning to ride a bicycle, drive a car, or speak in public, this is also stressful. Once the skills have been acquired, the stress abates; and the conscious effort required to perform skillfully is perfectly manageable.

The internal stresses argument can take another form. The argument goes like this: If I am having constantly to hide my "true" feelings and lay on a "contrived" display of overt behavior when I am interacting with people, day in day out, this will cause such a build up of internal tensions that sooner or later something will have to give. Notice that this argument tends to assume that stress results from the effort required to arrange behavior so that it does not reflect underlying feelings and emotions. It is certainly true that when there is a poor match between feelings and behavior the effort required to bottle up the feelings is wearing. But an interactively skilled person is not likely to be in this situation as often as an unskilled one. For a start the skilled person, by definition, finds it easier, and therefore *less* stressful, to control behavior. Secondly, the skilled person is much clearer about *when* to control behavior and when not to. In other words, internal stresses are *reduced* as you become more skillful. Furthermore, the skillful, insightful practitioner of interactive skills understands that his interactions with people *are* frequently going to be stressful and he plans "safe" ways of releasing the stresses. A quota of sports and pastimes, planned relaxation, some form of meditation perhaps—all these and many others can be used to work off the stresses and ensure that behavior in face to face encounters is nicely controlled and compatible with whatever the objectives of the occasion are.

One final point on stress: A main source of cumulative stress is failure itself—the constant bruising effect of failing to achieve your objectives, the nagging suspicion that you could have handled that better, the unplesant ambiguity of not being able to put your finger on what went wrong—or even *if* something *did* go wrong. These are the stuff of which stress is made. An interactively skilled person has a better "hit rate" in terms of achieving objectives in interaction than an unskilled person. The better the hit rate, the less the stress. An interactively skilled person even considers failure to be an opportunity to learn; and this quest to learn from mistakes and actively strive for improvement cushions the bruising still further.

Another frequent objection to the suggestion that behavior be consciously organized and controlled is that to do so would not be fair to other people. How would the people on the receiving end of our behavior know the "real" us? Would they be confused if we behaved differently on different occasions? Would they suspect that we were nongenuine or inconsistent? Worse still, would they condemn us as guilty of manipulation and Machiavellian practices? Two points need to be made here. First, the bit of us that is real to other people *is* our behavior because, as we have already established, it is visible. So, however we behave, it is real to other people. Secondly, worries about manipulation and inconsistency tend to abate when you realize that interactive skills tend to push for increased openness and explicitness in relationships with people. This is the reverse of the connotations that most people have in connection with manipulation. Manipulation is considered by most people to be a furtive, clandestine way of influencing people. Innocent victims are engineered into something and—this is an important ingredient of manipulation also—realize *afterwards* what happened: too late to avert it but early enough to resent it.

Such goings-on are nothing whatever to do with the proper use of interactive skills. Interactive skills are not about being furtive; they are about being transparent. They are not about confusing people and keeping them in the dark; they are about behaving clearly and in so doing getting clear behaviors in return. They are not about hidden motives and facades but about explicit objectives and authentic, in step behaviors.

Let us explore one final objection before going on to spend the remainder of this chapter establishing the links between situations, objectives, and behavior.

An objection often levelled is: How can we be expected to organize and plan our behavior? We don't have time! We spend too much time planning already and all to no avail; more often than not, we have to ditch the plan because it turns out to be unrealistic anyway.

The theoretical answer to this is that planning actually saves time in the end. Instead of unproductive, rambling meetings, planning helps to cut the overall time and push up productivity. But the problem with this sort of answer is that people react by claiming that they have not even the time to invest in the initial planning necessary to reap the eventual reward of time savings. It is rather like giving someone with no capital advice about how they could invest their money profitably if only they had some. A more realistic way of overcoming the objection is to show that planning is *not* synonymous with preparing. Planning can only be done beforehand if we have time to do it and if we have sufficient advance information on which to base the plan. Quite clearly, when it comes to the business of interacting with other people, these two prerequisites are often not met. Countless interactions spring up spontaneously and many can develop into interactions of a crucial nature. It is commonplace to hear that all the vital decisions are taken in the dining room over lunch, or during casual encounters in corridors, or even in lavatories! Frequently, then, we are unprepared in the sense that we have not had a chance to plan beforehand.

Beforehand planning is not the only sort of planning there is. It is quite possible to plan in a much more on-going, dynamic sense; and this is far more important in the rough and tumble of face to face interactions than static, preparatory planning activities. On-going planning requires us to size up the situation *as we are in it*, with the interaction already developing. It requires us to think actively about what we want to achieve within the life of the interaction, and how best to arrange our visible behavior so that we are successful. This sort of planning does not call for any extra time. It merely requires a more disciplined conscious approach during interactions. It also requires us to be equally alert to behavioral issues and content issues in parallel, a skill that we shall pinpoint more carefully in a later chapter.

This emphasis on on-going planning does not exclude the possibility of beforehand planning. You may have many interactions where you know about them in advance and have sufficient information to do some preparatory planning. You may frequently instigate interactions yourself, for example, rather than participating in discussions initiated by other people. You may have advance notice of key interactions where you judge that it is crucial to plan your approach beforehand. Typical examples might include a salesman calling on a likely prospect, a personnel manager preparing for a tricky negotiation, a job candidate going to a selection interview, a manager preparing to evaluate one of his subordinates.

The remainder of this book proceeds on the assumption that you believe your behavior to be an important enough factor in your people dealings to want to get better at consciously organizing and controlling it.

THE LINKS BETWEEN SITUATIONS, OBJECTIVES, AND BEHAVIOR

The concept to be introduced in this section falls into the "You know it makes sense" category. Conceptually, people have little trouble in both absorbing it and subscribing to it. Furthermore, the concept is not new. The snag, in common with most "You know it makes sense" concepts, is in actually doing it. It is patently obvious that there is often such a wide gulf between *knowing* something and doing it that many people fail to bridge it. Frequently, heavy smokers, for example, will accept that smoking is damaging to health, but continue to do it. Compulsive eaters will accept that their eating habits cause weight problems, but continue to eat between meals. The difference between knowing and doing is evident in many aspects of human behavior: highway "madness," not wearing seat belts, not using time fruitfully enough, not saving energy, not observing proven safety precautions—the list is endless. Knowing is clearly not in itself a sufficient prerequisite for doing.

The warning, then, is that the concept that follows

requires practical skill to translate it beyond mere knowledge into action. That said, let us look at the concept itself.

We have already had to qualify much of the discussion on behavior by pointing out what is appropriate behaviorally depends intimately on other factors. The simple truth is that behavior does not make sense unless it is viewed within the confines of a specific set of circumstances. It follows that behavior is, at best, a *means*, and that for the *ends* we need to look beyond behavior itself.

The total framework is, first, to be in touch with the reality of the "people" situations we encounter; secondly, to be clear about what objectives it is realistic to attempt to achieve; and thirdly, to be able to arrange behavior so that it is in step with those objectives. Rather than develop this in the abstract, here is an example to show how it is possible to use this framework to link the circumstances of a situation, objectives, and behavior together in a tight bond.

The situation first: Suppose that you have just taken over as manager from a colleague who considered that he was not doing his job properly unless he *told* his subordinates what to do and scrutinized closely to check that they did it. Your first impressions are that your predecessor's behavior style had had the effect of stifling ideas among your new team. This is a disappointment to you because you want them to be aware that you not only welcome but expect ideas and suggestions from them. You decide to set about opening up communications between you and them so that they can become less wary of committing themselves and more forward in producing ideas. Furthermore, you decide to get this process started by inviting your direct reports to a meeting.

Obviously, in real life you would know much more than the bare bones this description of the situation offers. You would, for example, know all sorts of extra points about the way the subordinates had behaved so far in interaction with you as their new boss. You would know some of the individual differences that were characteristic of them.

The next step is to allow the circumstances of this situation to contaminate your decisions about what objective you will strive to achieve in the meeting. Opinions on how far you can go in one initial get-together with your direct reports will vary, depending on all sorts of differences in emphasis and perception that we make in our reading of the situation just described. Some will feel it best to soft-pedal and just have a relaxing "getting to know each other better" type of meeting. Others will judge that to be an unambitious flavor for the meeting and want to pitch in immediately with more specific objectives and a more tangible output. More will be said about the process of judging what it is realistic to achieve in the next chapter, where we focus attention on objectives.

Here is an example of the sort of objective you might decide to aim for in the circumstances of the situation just described.

> To run the meeting in such a way that my subordinates have been encouraged to come up with lots of ideas and suggestions.
> I shall have achieved this successfully if:
> a. Each subordinate present has produced at least three suggestions by the end of the meeting.
> b. We have agreed that at least half the suggestions are worthy of further exploration/action.
> c. The meeting finishes within one and a half hours of its starting time.
> d. At least a third of the participants spontaneously remark that the meeting has been useful/rewarding/involving and the like.

Notice that this objective is couched in fairly specific terms and pinpoints the state of affairs that we wish to exist by the time the meeting ends. The merits of this sort of construction, or housestyle, will be discussed in Chapter Four. Meanwhile your attention should be drawn to the immediacy of the objective. It relates to the interaction itself and only has a one and a half hour life. This is a vital characteristic because we want the objective to guide us in deciding how to behave during this particular face to face interaction. If the objective was more far reaching or more general, it is unlikely that it would circumscribe behavior adequately.

The final step in the process is to think about how best to behave in order to maximize the probability of achieving the objective. Here is an example of a behavior approach that is in step with the objective.

> Since they are unlikely to be able to respond spontaneously to any pleas from me for suggestions, I'll give them plenty of advance warning about the meeting. I will deliberately choose a topic for the meeting where the likelihood that they will have lots of reasonable ideas is high. I'll circulate news of the topic, together with the suggestion that they think about it beforehand and come to the meeting with some ideas at the ready. At the meeting, I'll start it off by asking them if they have any ideas on "measures" that we could apply to our current meeting to judge its success together at the conclusion. If they haven't any ideas on this, then I'll put one up, tentatively, as a trial balloon, hoping to spark off some further suggestions from them. I'll adopt a similar strategy over the plan for how the meeting should proceed; asking them for suggestions first and, only if that fails, putting some forward myself. Whenever they put forward a suggestion, I'll react to it in a positive way by supporting it or seeking clarification to get some aspect clearer. I will not disagree with any suggestions during this particular meeting nor will I play devil's advocate, however tempting that reaction might be. I'll write all their suggestions down and read them back to check that I have understood/recorded them correctly. At the conclusion of the meeting, I will invite them to join me in applying the success measures which we agreed upon at the outset, and, in particular, to check on whether at least half the recorded suggestions are worthy of further exploration/action.

Every bit of this plan is heavily contaminated by the objective. The behavioral stance will need to be mainly seeking and supportive. Telling behaviors and other sorts of reactions are to be curbed lest they jeopardize the accomplishment of the objective. It will therefore be necessary throughout the meeting consciously to control behavior so that it remains in step with the objective.

The problems of keeping behavior in step with objectives are very real. I know that I frequently catch my behavior drifting beyond the parameters set by the objective I am aiming for. This is not too difficult to spot in others, too, providing you have some inkling of their objective. Here are some examples observed recently.

> The personnel director who met me in order to assess my capabilities in relation to an assignment he was setting up. He actually started our meeting by saying, quite explicitly, that he wanted to spend an hour or so learning about my experience/expertise and not spending much time describing the problem/assignment as he saw it on this occasion. Two hours later I was still trying to get a word in edgeways!

> The salesman who solemnly told me that whenever he was faced with a prospect who was a "low reactor" (someone who neither agrees nor disagrees but just plays it deadpan), his tactic was to step up his rate of open-ended questioning and to tolerate relatively long pauses, thus "forcing" the client to react. When I accompanied him on some sales calls, I found he did the exact opposite! He stepped *up* his sales patter, dropped his questioning rate and filled every silence by talking nineteen to the dozen.

> The manager who started a problem-solving meeting by saying how important it was to talk all round the problem and to respect everyone's different points of view and so forth, and then proceeded to bamboozle everyone into his way of thinking, shooting down alternative views of the problem and effectively gagging everyone present.

> The personnel manager who told me how important it was for him to gain personal credibility with the line managers with whom he was about to have a session and went on to blind and bore them with personnel jargon.

Examples of the difficulty of keeping behavior in step with objectives extend beyond face to face encounters. Politicians are often suspect on this count. People are frequently at a loss to square political actions with the declared objectives. When President Ford pardoned ex-President Nixon, for example, there was an uproar because people saw this as a piece of behavior that was out of step with the objective declared by President Ford: that it was his priority to restore confidence in the White House administration by being seen to be straight and honest in all their dealings. These sorts of out of stepness lead to credibility gaps, an erosion of trust, and to sinister reputations based on assumptions of deceit and double-dealing. If the observed behavior is out of step with the declared objectives, then only two conclusions are possible. The most charitable is that the person is unable to control his behavior so that it is in step with his objectives. The other is that the person has hidden objectives that differ from the ones he declared and that the private objectives are more instrumental in shaping his behavior than the public ones.

BEHAVIOR AND OBJECTIVES: IN STEP AND OUT OF STEP RELATIONSHIPS

Let us explore this concept of objectives and behavior by using a blow by blow transcript of an interaction. In the excerpt that follows, David is personnel director. Two of his subordinates are present. Chris has been in personnel for many years, but has only recently been appointed manager of a new unit called the Organization Development Center (ODC). Fred is the personnel director's administrative assistant.

As you will see, they are meeting a little in advance of a scheduled meeting between them and George, the company's director of training, and Ian, who is manager of the management training unit (MTU).

As you read through the transcript of the conversation, try to decide which contributions are in step and which out of step with the following objectives:

> *David's objective:*
> To have agreed what they want to achieve in the meeting with George and Ian.
> David would have been successful if:
> a. They had agreed that the objective was to sort out the boundaries between the ODC and MTU.
> b. He had secured Chris's agreement to postpone any ideas of amalgamating the ODC and MTU.
>
> *Chris's objective:*
> To have got David's agreement to allocate both extra accommodation and extra help for the ODC.
> Chris would have been successful if:
> a. David had sanctioned Chris's request for a conference room.
> b. David has named one of his other direct reports as the person to help out on one of the projects.

With these objectives in mind, here is a verbatim account of what was said.

> **1. DAVID**   All right, Chris, we've got just 15 minutes or so to talk about this afternoon's meeting before George and Ian get here. Where do you want to come out of it?
>
> **2. CHRIS**   Just before we do that, I wanted to have a word about accommodation for the OD center. You remember I sent you a memo on it. . . .
>
> **3. DAVID**   Look! I'm under enough pressure to cut down on the ODC in its initial stages as it is without you asking for a whole suite of conference rooms.
>
> **4. CHRIS**   I'm not asking for a suite of rooms, only for one biggish conference room where senior clients can meet in an atmosphere conducive to problem-solving.

5. DAVID Well, I'm warning you that the ODC image is a luxury I can't afford just now. Personnel's budget is under fire. We're likely to have to absorb a 10 per cent cut at any minute.

6. CHRIS Well, you know my views on that. If the president squeezes the personnel function any harder, there won't be a worthwhile service left. He's cutting off his nose to spite his face.

7. DAVID Okay, okay. Let's talk about that another time. Now, what about this afternoon's meeting? Right now I don't feel clear enough about what we want to get out of it.

8. CHRIS So I can't change your mind about accommodation for the ODC?

9. DAVID I thought I'd made it clear. If you are responsible for setting up a project, you are also responsible for housing it. Fight it out with the others along that corridor. If you can persuade them they need less space then you can have your conference room.

10. CHRIS But that's not fair! I have never gained the impression that I was supposed to *fight* for office accommodation that the ODC *must* have if it is to function properly. Once you had backed the center, agreed its budget, and so on, I naturally assumed that other necessary facilities would be forthcoming.

11. DAVID I consider this whole issue to be a very small point within the total compass of what has to be achieved. You don't need to bring these small problems to me.

12. CHRIS Well, I'm sorry, but I don't see it as a small problem. If the center isn't housed adequately then it can't function properly and that's all there is to it.

13. FRED If you want me to come and act as a referee between you and the others I'll gladly do so, but I'm inclined to agree that it's a relatively small point.

14. DAVID Good. Now let's move on.

15. CHRIS I just hope you've registered my disapproval

over the handling of this whole thing. When I took on this job, I naturally assumed that I would have sufficient support to make it viable. . . .

16. DAVID In this climate, you can't afford to assume anything. I don't, and so I can't see why you should be able to. I continue to hold you totally responsible for the establishment of a successful organization development center.

17. CHRIS While we're on the subject, that brings me to another point. The sales engineering project has got to the point where it needs an extra pair of hands. I can't chair all the workshops myself. It means that other projects aren't getting enough attention.

18. DAVID Why don't you get the two personnel managers involved? Tim Brown in sales and Stephen Jones in engineering? You can't do it *for* them. All we can expect the center to do is *start* projects of that kind. But once they are launched they should be handed over to the local personnel people.

19. CHRIS Yes, but both Tim and Stephen are already complaining of being over-committed without this. They are too busy fire fighting on the industrial relations front to have time left to resource a project like this.

20. DAVID Then perhaps that tells us something.

21. CHRIS Like what? That the personnel managers are busy doing the wrong things?

22. DAVID No. That if personnel managers are busy with the short term you have got a problem in winning some of their time for a longer term project like the sales engineering one.

23. CHRIS Well, with all due respect, we all know that already. Surely the trick is to see how short term needs can be dealt with to long term advantage?

24. FRED Or to take long term issues and make them attractive in the short term?

25. DAVID It has to be that way or else we shall be accused of not working for the good of the business: just for our own professional self-interest. We are under enough pressure as it is.

26. CHRIS   Well, I'm telling you that *I'm* under pressure to find someone to chair those meetings! I don't think I'll succeed in getting either Tim or Stephen to take it on somehow.

27. DAVID   Look! I'm definitely going to have to make choices about the deployment of resources in personnel HQ. If the personnel managers in the divisions are asking for extra help on industrial relations and compensation issues. . . well, let's put it this way. . . we must put the resources where the pressure is.

28. CHRIS   I think you've changed your views on the role of personnel HQ and the divisions.

29. DAVID   Well, it's clear that we haven't yet convinced the divisional personnel managers about the need for the OD center. I've always been clear that HQ has a dual role: to provide support to the divisions *and* to look ahead and have some forward plans. As far as I'm concerned we need an OD center, but we are going to have it with the blessing of the divisional personnel managers. That's your priority. If it takes another year just getting their support, it will be worth it.

30. DAVID'S SEC.   Excuse me, sorry to interrupt, but George is here. Are you ready for him?

31. DAVID   Just hang on to him for a minute or two, will you, Sue? Now come on, Chris, we haven't planned this meeting at all. What do you want to achieve?

32. CHRIS   I thought it was your meeting. You called it, after all. What objectives did you have in mind?

33. DAVID   I thought we needed it to clear up the boundaries between your center and George's management training team. Weren't you complaining of overlaps and fuzzy terms of reference?

34. CHRIS   Well, I don't know if I'd put it as strongly as complaining—but I do think it would help to try and straighten out who is supposed to do what — yes.

35. DAVID So how do you want to play it? I'd be inclined to sit George next to me and let him tell us all about it. I agree that we've got to get the responsibilities of the center and management training sorted out. Just because the center has got off to rather a shaky start that's no reason to have management training tarred with the same brush. I feel duty bound to point this out to George. We're ready for them now, aren't we?

36. FRED I wouldn't have thought so, but we can't keep them waiting any longer. Shall I fetch them in?

37. CHRIS Just a minute. I've got a feeling that we aren't agreed at all. Listening to what you've just said. David . . . it leaves me wondering why we are having this meeting at all. Are we going to suggest that the center and management training amalgamate or not? I thought that was the original idea.

38. DAVID Lord, no! I'm saying that we can't do that now because of the poor reputation of the center. If it had got off to a better start, that would have been a different matter. . . quite a different matter. I now think it's a better idea to leave them separated organizationally but to work out the overlaps and so on. Get them in please, Fred.

How did David and Chris fare in your estimation? Do you agree that neither was very successful in achieving his objectives? David failed to get the objectives for the meeting with George and Ian agreed, and he was certainly nowhere near to securing Chris's agreement to no amalgamation, as we see from Chris's outburst in 37. With quite different objectives, Chris hasn't done too well, either. He came away without a conference room and without one of David's direct reports assigned to the sales engineering project.

What went wrong? Probably at least three things.

First, the two men had quite different objectives. This meant that in a short time like 15 minutes there was a struggle over whose objectives should dominate. Different though they were, given a longer interaction, both sets of objectives could have been achieved. In the circumstances, you might feel that one of the protagonists should have backed off in the interests of *some* progress. I agree, and feel it should have been Chris, since it became clear very quickly that the accomplishment of his objectives was unlikely in the circumstances. In fact, the more he strove to achieve them, the more certain was his failure. This means that his failure was, in part, due to having a poor judgment about the objectives it was feasible to go for within the circumstances of the situation.

Secondly, too many of David's behaviors were out of step with his objective. He started out in step (1) and he finished more or less in step (31, 33, 35, and 37), but he allowed the influence of Chris's behavior to push him into an out of step position for most of the time (3, 5, 9, 11, 16, 18, 20, 22, 25, 27, and 29). He tried to get back in step a couple of times (7 and 14), but Chris always managed to drag him off course again. My final balance sheet for David shows that out of 18 behaviors only 7 were in step. I conclude that he deserved to fail. It wasn't just Chris's fault.

Thirdly, far too many of Chris's behaviors were out of step with his objective. He, like David, also started out in step (2 and 4) but *starting* in step is relatively easy. It is *keeping* in step that is difficult. He slips out of step very quickly, falling an easy prey to some of his pet gripes and hobby horses (6, 21, 23, and 28 are the most flagrant examples). When you remember that Chris's objectives were all about securing David's agreement and cooperation in various ways, it is easy to see that many of his reactions to David were badly out of step (10, 12, 15, 19, and 26). Overall, in the passage up to 30, where David's secretary interrupts to say that George is waiting, Chris only has four of his 13 behaviors in step (2, 4, 8, and 17); and, of these, 4 and 8 are suspect if we take other behavioral nuances into account.

Both men did badly if we merely view their behavior against their own personal objectives. By the time we view their behavior in interaction, with different objectives pulling them in different directions, the result is an unsatisfactory failure for both. Both men are responsible. Either of them could have used more in step behaviors to have salvaged the situation.

In the next chapter, there are two more transcripts to give you practice in using objectives as a backdrop for identifying in step and out of step behaviors.

One of the transcripts traces David through the meeting with George and Ian. The other introduces new characters and is based on an appraisal discussion situation.

SUMMARY

The chapter opened by declaring four basic assumptions that underpin the interactive skills approach: that behavior in face to face encounters does affect the outcome; that behavior needs to vary from situation to situation; that behavior should be in step with objectives; that behavior frequently needs to be consciously organized and controlled.

Some of the common objections to these assumptions—particularly the last—were explored. Issues touched on were the honesty/dishonesty of having underlying feelings that were not expressed in overt behavior; the problem of internal stress arising from the effort needed consciously to maintain a particular display of overt behavior; the problem of manipulation and inconsistency in our dealings with people. Finally, the problems of finding time to plan and organize behavior.

The remainder of the chapter was spent showing how situations, objectives, and behavior itself act as a complex system where alterations in any one inevitably has repercussions for the others. In particular, the idea that there should be a vital bond between objectives and behavior was explored. A number of illustrations were used to show how judgments about the appropriateness of behavior can be made in the light of objectives.

3

Case Studies on In Step and Out of Step Behavior Recognition

This chapter is devoted to two case studies in the form of transcripts. The idea is to give you further practice in relating behavior to objectives before moving on to look at both objectives and behavior in more detail in subsequent chapters.

Of course, there are limitations to this sort of case study approach. Unlike real life, transcripts are in writing, and this both helps and hinders the analytical process. It *helps* by having everything captured in writing so that we look back at what was said as many times as we wish. It *hinders* because the verbatim account only tells us what was said and starves us of other accompanying behavioral information that we have access to in real life. Intonation, for example, facial expressions, and the whole gamut of nonverbal behaviors are largely left to the imagination.

The other major limitation is that these case studies are exclusively about *other people* and not about ourselves. The skill of spotting in step and out of step behavior in others is not an adequate replacement for the skill needed to monitor and control our own behavioral performance. This you can only practice in your real-life interactions. Later chapters will show you how to work out objectives, how to plan behavior, and how to monitor behavior. For the time being, the practical rule of thumb, or technique, is consciously and continually to ask yourself two questions: "What do I want to achieve in this interaction?" and, "Is my behavior in step with it?" If your answer to the first is "I don't know," "I'm not sure," or "I don't want to achieve anything, really," then you need not bother with the second question at all. If you are not consciously aware of wishing to achieve an objective, then you can afford to freewheel behaviorally. This is because you can neither be in nor out of step with no objectives. One word of warning: If you find that for, say, a quarter of your interactive time you have no objectives and are accordingly behaviorally listless, you are in trouble. Such a high level of purposeless activity should be questioned, and I shall take this up in the next chapter along with some other crucial issues connected directly with objectives and indirectly with behavior.

FIRST CASE STUDY

Let us follow the characters we introduced in the last chapter through the second part of their meeting. You will remember that David, the personnel director, and Chris, manager of the newly established organization development center, were preparing to interact with George, director of training, and Ian, manager of the management training unit. Throughout the verbatim account that follows, concentrate on analyzing David's behavior, using the following objectives as your frame of reference:

David's objective:
To have defined the responsibilities of the ODC and MTU in such a way that everyone is clear and cooperation between the two units is more likely.

David will have been successful if:

a. The main responsibilities of ODC and MTU have been listed and areas of potential overlap identified.

b. He has specifically said that he doesn't think it appropriate to merge ODC and MTU at present.

c. George and/or Ian have volunteered to work with him and/or Chris on at least one specific project or activity.

d. George and Ian leave the meeting making unsolicited remarks about how useful it has been in clearing the air, tidying up grey areas, and the like.

With this objective in mind analyze David's behavior in the following transaction:

[Enter George and Ian]

1. DAVID Sorry to have kept you waiting, gentlemen.

2. GEORGE That's all right. It's really been quite useful. Given Ian and myself time to collect our wits.

3. DAVID Fine. Well, would you like to start off? What can we do for you?

4. GEORGE Best if Ian explains, I think. He's the guy who's done the homework.

5. IAN Oh dear! What a build up. Well, as I understand it we are here to work out what to do to educate management throughout the company—overseas as well as here—so that they understand the president's management style. A number of ideas have been bandied around, ranging from the suggestion that the president runs a series of seminars himself to the suggestion that someone studies his style closely enough to become an authority on it!

6. GEORGE Yes, that puts it very fairly, I think. The president is certainly eager to find some economical way of getting his philosophy across. He seems pretty exasperated that people don't read him more easily.

7. DAVID In my view, there is no substitute for an

eyeball to eyeball encounter for this sort of thing. Best thing would be to have the president sort this out with his direct reports and then have it cascade down in a series of workshops. As a matter of fact, we did this in the personnel department when I took over. We had him here for a couple of hours while we quizzed him. It worked very well, didn't it, Fred?

8. FRED   Yes, everyone thought it very valuable. We taped it all too, so there is a transcript of the whole thing. Would that be an idea, I wonder? How about getting the president to do a video cassette? It means he only needs to do the session once and it could go out to all the overseas territories.

9. IAN   Would he be prepared to produce a video?

10. GEORGE   Oh, I would think so. If we put it to him the right way. I should think he'd be rather flattered.

11. DAVID   I've got my doubts. The president doesn't spend time *talking* about a philosophy of management. He only ever talks about specific managerial problems. I just can't envisage anyone getting him to sustain a conversation on something as general as his management style—or anyone else's, for that matter.

12. IAN   So what would you suggest, then, David?

13. DAVID   Perhaps we could feed him some questions aimed at getting his views on some specific problems. If we chose the questions carefully, his answers could provide the clues we need on the more general aspects of his attitudes, style, and what-have-you.

14. CHRIS   In my experience, telling him he has some problems isn't very successful. His attitude seems to be "I don't have any problems. My subordinates have the problems."

15. DAVID   I wasn't suggesting that we tell him he has problems. I was merely proposing that we draw up a list of questions that are carefully designed to reveal his management style without directly appearing to do so.

16. CHRIS   I think he'd be smart enough to see through that.

17. GEORGE   So what do *you* think would work. Chris? It sounds as if you don't favor the president being involved at all?

18. CHRIS   No, I don't, really. I think it would be best to have someone track the president through a number of ordinary working days, observing his style until such time as he—the observer, that is—can pinpoint the salient features of his approach and draw up a program to explain it to others.

19. IAN   Who would be the best person to take on such a project?

20. DAVID   Well, I personally think that someone from your management training unit would be best qualified for that sort of assignment, Ian.

21. GEORGE   Yes, Ian's people have clocked up a lot of experience on various tracking assignments.

22. CHRIS   Would it seem a little odd that this was a personnel project being carried out by someone from *outside* the personnel department?

23. FRED   Well, I don't think anyone has designated this as a personnel project exactly. Would it matter whether it was headed up in personnel or in training? I can't think that it would. So long as the objective is achieved, what does it matter?

24. DAVID   I'd certainly like to propose that you take it on, Ian, in conjunction with Chris here. Surely this would be a good opportunity to cooperate?

25. CHRIS   Well, I'm sorry. I quite definitely think this is one for the OD center. When it was set up, we made it quite clear that it would operate at director level in the company. I need hardly point out that the president *is* a director level client! It will only cause confusion if an assignment of this kind goes to another unit.

26. DAVID   I wasn't suggesting that Ian's people do it in isolation. I think it important that this is tackled as a joint project. You need to get together to work it out, to cooperate, decide who is going to do what, and so on. I strongly urge that the actual tracking—if it comes to that—is done by Ian or one of his people. We need to tap their sort of expertise on a job like this.

27. IAN   How do you mean "if it comes to that?" I was under the impression that we had agreed to tackle this as a tracking assignment.

28. DAVID   Well, at this stage I'd rather leave the options open. As far as I'm concerned, I leave it to you and Chris to come up with proposals.

29. GEORGE   Hang on, then! Does that mean we are any further forward? I thought *this* meeting was supposed to agree on a course of action. What's the use of postponing it? We'll only need to meet a second time to consider the proposals.

30. DAVID   I'm only suggesting that as a way forward because we don't seem to be agreed on any one definitive way of going about this. It also seems to me to be a golden opportunity to get these two working together for once instead of arguing about who does what. We all work for the same company, after all.

31. IAN   Well, I'm happy to work closely with Chris on this, but I feel it is important to clear up some of the ambiguity by appointing a project leader. Is that to be Chris or myself, or someone else?

32. DAVID   Well, in view of the fact that the OD center has more organizational prestige, I would suggest Chris heads it up. This could be a useful forerunner to actual amalgamation between the two units.

33. GEORGE   Sorry. Who said anything about amalgamation? As I've told you before, that'll happen over my dead body and not before. Anyway, we didn't come here to talk about that. Are we agreed on this president thing then?

34. DAVID   I'm surprised you come out so strongly against joining the two units together, George. I see it as a considerable advantage to both sides. It enhances the OD center and provides them with manpower and skills they need. It also gets the management training unit reporting in at an appropriate level. I'm sure Ian here would be glad to see that.

35. IAN   That's as may be, but at present I'd rather confine this discussion to the immediate project in hand. I think the reporting relationships must be sorted out at your level.

36. DAVID   Come on, Ian. You're fencing. Do you want to join the center or not? I think it's important that we establish that.

37. IAN   Let's put it this way. I'm certainly glad that you've set up a center here at HQ. I think it's got an important job to do. No doubt about that. On the other hand, the management training team has been in existence for five or six years now, earning a reputation all over the company for sound, helpful work. That reputation has been hard won.

38. GEORGE   I think that's quite enough on this subject just now. I agree with Ian. It's something that you and I need to sort out, David, one day when the center has established itself. Are we done, then?

39. DAVID   I wouldn't want to leave Ian and Chris with the impression that we weren't at one on this one, George. I'm sure you agree that the amalgamation of the two units is highly desirable from the company's point of view? We have discussed this before, and I thought that was our joint view?

40. GEORGE   Look! I thought I'd already made it clear that I don't want to discuss this now. In fact I'd go further, David, and say that I think it unfair of you to have introduced this without due warning. As far as we are concerned, this meeting was convened to plan ways and means of introducing the president's style to the rest of the company.

41. DAVID   Very well. I can't help but comment that this is a pity in my view. We specifically had this issue of the center and management training on our agenda. I feel that the plans for them to cooperate over the presidential project lead us inevitably into discussion about the way the two units interface. To be prepared to discuss one and not the other is hardly logical. But still. . .if that's the way you want it.

42. GEORGE   Well, I've got to go! I didn't think we were going to talk about this today. Got to be somewhere else in a few minutes anyway. . .

43. DAVID   Okay. So long as we agree that it is important to work out the roles of the two units. We need to work together on a common charter. Close liaison to refine the boundaries is essential. No one ever plans to duplicate, you know. Duplication is always in the past tense. The danger is to leave these questions unanswered.

44. IAN   I'll get together with Chris, then. Did we agree which of us was to lead the project?

45. CHRIS   Yes. I thought it was agreed that I should.

46. DAVID   Fine. I look forward to hearing your proposals. An important project. No doubt about that. The president is a difficult man in many ways. If we can get people throughout the company adjusted to his thinking, blending their styles in with his. . .well, it'll make a vast difference. . .a vast difference.

[Exit George and Ian]

47. FRED   Well, I don't know about you, but I thought that was a difficult meeting in many ways.

48. DAVID   Difficult? How do you mean? I thought we were pretty successful, considering.

49. CHRIS   But I thought you said we weren't going to raise the question of amalgamation at this stage?

50. DAVID   Well. . .the time seemed right. It's important to play these things by ear to some extent, you know. I think it worked pretty well. We've got you appointed as project leader. What more do you want?

51. CHRIS   I didn't get the impression that Ian was particularly happy about that.

52. DAVID   Oh, come on, now! It's all been agreed. You've had a lot of my time this afternoon already. . .

53. FRED   Come on, Chris. David has had enough of us for now. We'll sort ourselves out all right later.

Once again David has largely failed to achieve the objective that we decided to analyze his performance against. The main responsibilities of ODC and MTU have not been listed or even talked through; he never made it clear that he didn't favor amalgamation—indeed George and Ian obviously got the impression that he did! Neither George nor Ian left the meeting remarking that it had been useful. Quite the reverse, in fact; George seemed rather annoyed. The only fragment of success is that there was agreement from Ian to work with Chris on the presidential project (31 and 44), but each time the agreement looked rather half baked and short of anything resembling enthusiasm, as Chris pointed out in 51.

Now, it is quite possible that we have misunderstood David's objective for the meeting. People's objectives are not visible unless they choose to make them so by *saying* what they are. The "evidence" for David's objective came in the earlier discussion with Chris and Fred (Chapter 2, pages 38–39, contributions 33, 35, and 38) but it may well be that he had hidden objectives that were more influential in shaping his behavior than the one we are using. If so, notice the effect that his behavior had. In the main, he was instrumental in causing considerable confusion, and, by the time George and Ian had left, Fred and Chris both admit to seeing difficulties. David, on the other hand, is either happy because his hidden objective had been achieved or is rationalizing his failure away (48, 50, and 52). This is a frequent ritual that people go through after interactions, and it is made easier if they do not disclose their objective until *after* the event. This means that whatever the outcome, they can adjust their objective to fit, and, accordingly, can guarantee success every time. It looks as if David is a skilled rationalizer!

Despite this, let us apply our in and out of step criterion to David's behavior, using the objective we, in our wisdom, dreamed up on his behalf! During the time that George and Ian were present, David produced 18 contributions. My analysis breaks down his behavior into six main clusters, as follows:

1, 3
David's starter behaviors. In the event, 3 was particularly unfortunate because it gave George and Ian "the floor," so to speak. This wouldn't have mattered except that it revealed a total misunderstanding about the objective for the meeting; 3 was out of step with David's objective. He would have done better to start with some sort of declaration of his objective and to have taken it from there. This would have brought the misunderstanding into the open from the outset and they could have made a deal: you help me to achieve my objective and I will help you to achieve yours.

7, 11, 13, 15
All are out of step with David's objective, but in step with George and Ian's. These behaviors could be forgiven if, subsequently, David had managed to get back in step with his own objective.

20, 24, 26
Possibly in step with the part of his objective having to do with securing a commitment to cooperation. But it is rather an obscure way of trying to achieve the objective, and it certainly causes Chris's resentment (22 and 25) and Ian's bid to secure clarity (27, 31, and 44). Weighing the matter, I will credit David with these behaviors and judge them to be more in step than out of step.

28, 30
Out of step, because the spirit of the objective was

very much to do with sorting things out in some detail there and then, within the compass of the meeting.

32, 34, 36, 39, 41

As out of step as out of step can be! The slide starts innocently enough with David's remark in 32; but, by the time he responds to George in 34, he has completely broken step with his own objective. A classic case of failing to control behavior so that it aligns adequately with the objective.

43, 46

A feeble attempt at recovery, but still out of step for the same reason that 28 and 30 were. David is shunting the detailed work on defining the responsibilities of the two units out of the meeting, when his objectives clearly envisaged that this would be a legitimate activity at the meeting.

Overall, then, my score sheet has a maximum of four of David's contributions in step (1, 20, 24, and 26), and I am hesitant about those, and the remaining 14 out of step. A poor behavioral performance that did nothing to avert failure.

SECOND CASE STUDY

This time the transcript that follows gives a verbatim account of an appraisal discussion between two men. They work in a large company's public relations department. Len is public relations director, and he is appraising Bob, who is one of his direct subordinates. They have worked together for many years and so tend to have a casual, friendly relationship. As you will see, Len is new to appraisal discussions in the more formal sense.

Please center attention on Len's behavior—again, to see how well it fits with the following objective:

Len's objective:

To have appraised Bob's performance in such a way that at least one plan for improved performance is agreed upon. Len will have been successful if:

a. At least one of the plans tightens up on the procedure for getting local press publicity throughout the country.

b. All the plans for improvement are in specific enough "action" terms to leave them in no doubt about what has to be done and by whom in the future.

c. Bob comes up with at least one plan for improvement himself.

d. Bob indicates that he has found the appraisal discussion useful/helpful.

e. He (Len) learns something about how he could improve his own performance as departmental head.

With this objective as the backdrop, analyze Len's behavior in the transcript.

[Len and Bob have been talking for some time about other matters when . . .]

1. LEN   Well, that just about wraps that up then, Bob. Have you anything else to add?

2. BOB   No, no. . .I'm quite clear about that. Leave it to me.

3. LEN   Fine. Er. . .Bob, you know this appraisal scheme they've been pushing lately?

4. BOB   Yes. I went to one of the presentations. It seemed like a good idea. Of course it isn't as applicable in our sort of work. But in principle I welcomed it.

5. LEN   How do you mean? What sort of work is it applicable to, then?

6. BOB   Oh, I'd have thought it was more useful in departments where the work is. . .you know, more tangible or more measurable.

7. LEN   Don't you think it's possible to put measures on our own activity, then, Bob?

8. BOB   Well, it depends what you mean by measures, doesn't it? If you mean objective things like how frequently we get favorable mentions in the press or the customer complaint levels—things like that—well, they are just trivial, aren't they? Missing the essence of the thing.

9. LEN   Hmm. I'm not so sure. Take the money-back guarantee launch. We agreed to get wide coverage in local newspapers throughout the country as well as all the TV and national press coverage. How well did we do on that?

10. BOB   Well, of course, the TV and national press coverage was admitted to be about the best we've ever had.

11. LEN   I know, I know. But I'm asking about our success in getting *local* coverage. If you remember, less glamorous local plugs were reckoned to be a key factor in getting people throughout the country to come and deal through us.

12. BOB   Yes, well, off hand, I'm not sure how we faired locally. We didn't really set up a scheme to monitor local press coverage, did we?

13. LEN   Didn't we? I thought that was implicit in that part of the plan.

14. BOB   Just a minute. Are you *getting* at me? Is this supposed to be an appraisal interview?

15. LEN   Well, yes. I must admit that I thought we would have a talk about your. . .our. . .performance. I hoped you might think it a good idea.

16. BOB   But we've been together for seven years now, and you've never had occasion to criticize me during that time.

17. LEN   I'm not criticizing you. If I've understood it right, appraising isn't so much about criticizing as about helping. I'm only raising the matter of the failure to get sufficient local press coverage in order to help improve future performance.

18. BOB   Well, I'm sorry Len, but I resent this. I didn't know this was to be an appraisal discussion, otherwise I would have prepared myself. It seems quite unfair for you to suddenly launch into a premeditated attack and expect me to defend myself. If that's what appraisal is about, let's forget it and go back to our normal way of carrying on.

19. LEN   Look, Bob. I've clearly not handled the opening of this session at all well. I didn't want to have you up in arms—quite the contrary in fact. I was anxious to keep this as informal and casual as possible.

20. BOB   Maybe I have overreacted a bit. It just seems a bit much to launch into an appraisal discussion after seven years of working closely together without any warning.

21. LEN   Okay, Bob, I'm sorry about that. Must admit I felt a bit embarrassed about the whole thing. But it's policy now, you know, and anyway I've been thinking about this appraisal business and it certainly seems to make sense. It's made me realize that I've been rather remiss in the past. Not giving people enough explicit feedback and help. Just being prepared to muddle along with half understandings and vague objectives.

22. BOB   I see what you are getting at. I've never had any trouble being clear about my objectives personally and I always feel that we understand each other pretty well, but other people in the department do complain that they have trouble being certain about what it is you want them to do precisely. Oh! I mustn't exaggerate, it doesn't come up all that often.

23. LEN   Often enough to explain some of my disappointments with people's performance, I bet.

24. BOB   How do you mean?

25. LEN   Well, let's go back to the example we were talking about earlier, Bob. When we agreed to go for wide coverage in the local press as well as nationally, I obviously *expected* certain things to happen. In the event, they didn't happen, or, at least, I don't think they did. So whose fault would you say that was?

26. BOB   I'm still very surprised that you keep bringing that up, Len. You had better come clean about what it was that you expected to happen, that didn't. I thought we'd done a good job on the money-back guarantee scheme. It's widely acknowledged that we did, anyway.

27. LEN   How about us doing it the other way around? If you'll tell me exactly what was done to ensure wide coverage in local papers, I'll promise to come clean about my disappointments.

28. BOB   Okay, Len. Well, as you know, our resources were pretty strained doing all the liaising with the national and trade press. Those press conferences take some organizing.

29. LEN   You're stalling again, Bob!

30. BOB   Oh, all right. I admit that I didn't think the local press campaign was anything like top priority. What difference would local coverage really have made anyway?

31. LEN   So, what *was* done, Bob?

32. BOB   Well, I think we sent out a memo to each of the branch managers urging them to push it with the local press in their respective areas.

33. LEN   A memo or a press release? Did we put "copy" into their hands?

34. BOB   Just a memo, I think. I expected the branch managers to see the advantages of getting local coverage in whatever way they thought appropriate. It's very difficult for us to know what makes attractive copy for the local press. It varies enormously from area to area.

35. LEN   Have we followed up to see how many branch managers *did* see the advantages?

36. BOB   No. I admit we haven't gotten around to that

yet. Anyway, surely it was up to them? *They* were free to push it or not as they felt fit?

37. LEN   You agree that one of our objectives was to get wide local press coverage in the launch program?

38. BOB   Yes. A low priority one, perhaps, but it was listed, yes.

39. LEN   So the question is, is it reasonable or even professional for us to simply delegate the actions necessary to achieve one of *our* objectives to the retail branch managers?

40. BOB   Just another example of the head office passing the buck, you mean?

41. LEN   Partly, partly. Look Bob, I know you're short staffed down there, but, in retrospect, what steps do you think you ought to have taken in the achievement of that objective?

42. BOB   We should have sent out a press release, I suppose. Then if the branch manager was busy or didn't feel like going to a lot of extra trouble, at least he could have passed the press release to the right quarter and left it at that.

43. LEN   Yes, I'm sure that would have been preferable. Branch managers just haven't got time to write their own copy. That's an example of how we as a department are supposed to help them, isn't it?

44. BOB   Can't argue about that one, Len. That's obviously quite right.

45. LEN   Could we agree that in future whenever we try to coordinate press coverage via line managers of any kind, we always take it upon ourselves to provide the copy?

46. BOB   Sure, yes. We should be doing that anyway.

47. LEN   So that can be adopted as a *measurable* aspect of future performance can it, Bob?

48. BOB   Hmm. I see what you're getting at.

49. LEN   I'm sure it's just a question of basic communications between us. If we can't communicate clearly in this, the PR department, I don't see much hope for us!

50. BOB   But talking of communications between us, Len, I was wondering. . .

51. LEN   Wondering what, Bob? If you've got any suggestions that'll help, please let's have them. It's all part of the appraisal, after all.

52. BOB   Well, I was wondering if you and I could spend longer at the outset of a project, defining it more precisely, allocating priorities, deciding who is going to do what, and so on. I honestly didn't realize that you thought local coverage on the guarantee project as important as you obviously did. Somehow there was a misunderstanding between us on that one, Len.

53. LEN   Hmm. We'll have to be careful that I don't finish up doing your job for you.

54. BOB   No, no, it's not that. Suppose, for example, we worked together, just at the start of new projects, on setting the objectives. Once they have been agreed between us, I'd expect to go off and decide on the best methods and so on to get the job done properly.

55. LEN   Yes. I see what you mean, that's back to objectives and measures again, isn't it? You're suggesting that we fashion the objectives and standards *together*, so that we have complete understanding—and then leave you to get on with the job within the agreed constraints?

56. BOB   Exactly! I'd certainly be happier if we went about it that way. You see, we do things so informally at the moment, I'm sure we leave lots unsaid that should be said. Think how often it transpires that I thought you were going to do something and you thought I was. . .it's a muddle.

57. LEN   Okay. Let's leave it at that, then. Let's agree that we'll use the new system for all future projects and that the onus is on you to come with some starter objectives and keep pinning me down till you're clear enough.

58. BOB   All right, Len, so long as you don't mind. Must admit that I've often wanted to do that but I thought you'd take offense, to be quite honest.

59. LEN   Perhaps this shows us the value of having these appraisal discussions. It certainly helps to direct attention on things like communication problems, doesn't it? Usually we're too busy with the job in hand to consider these other issues. But they're important, aren't they?

60. BOB   They certainly are. In fact, it's difficult to separate them out from the job itself. Obviously *how* you set the project up with me, the objectives we agree upon, and so on are vital elements in determining its success, aren't they?

61. LEN   We are agreed, then. I hope you didn't think I was being too critical earlier on, Bob? Overall, I think you know that I know you do a good professional job. I certainly wouldn't want this discussion to have given you a different impression.

62. BOB   No, no. I'm glad we've talked like this. In fact, I must say this appraisal business seems more applicable to us than I thought at first. Very useful, really very useful.

By my reckoning, Len has been successful in achieving the objective. He got the issue of press releases for local papers thoroughly aired and agreed upon (Bob's behavior in 42 and 44, for example). Bob explicitly comments on the usefulness of the discussion (62), and comes up with a suggestion for improvement himself (52). Furthermore, the discussion has resulted in Len learning about an improvement area for his own performance (55 and 57). All in all, a perfect match between the objective and the outcome.

So Len has been successful in achieving his ends. Now, let us look at the means he employed. Here is my in step, out of step analysis, starting with 3, since contributions 1 and 2 are the tailpiece of the last interaction and not relevant to the appraisal.

3, 5, 7, 9, 11, 13

These must be judged, as a very oblique opening to the appraisal. They are in step with the part of the objective to do with press releases for the local media but out of step with other parts of the objective that call for the appraisal discussion to be openly acknowledged as such. For example, it is difficult to see how Len hoped to get Bob to comment favorably on the appraisal procedure if he (Bob) never knew that was what it was! All in all, Len opens with a string of out of step behaviors.

15, 17, 19, 21

This is the phase of the interaction where Len is forced, by Bob's behavior, to "come clean" about it being an appraisal! In a sense, these are "changing step" behaviors that result in Len adjusting his behavior sufficiently to be fully in step by 21. Overall, Len's behavior in this part of the exchange was in step, but only because Bob forced the issue.

23–49

Fourteen consecutive behaviors all nicely in step with the objective, culminating in specific agreement between the two men.

51, 53, 55, 57

The phase of the discussion where the tables are turned and Bob produces his suggestion aimed at improving Len's behavior. My only out of step question is 53, which I consider a risky behavior in the light of the fact that Len wanted to learn something to his own advantage. His reaction in 53 could have dampened the suggestion down rather than encouraged it. In the event, Bob pressed his point home, and Len got back in step again by 55.

59, 61

Rounding off behaviors by Len, both in step with the part of his objective to do with giving Bob a good feeling about it all.

In summary, Len was very successful in achieving his objective—and deservedly so, since out of a total of 30 behaviors, 23 were completely in step. Only the opening sequence, where Len tried to manipulate Bob into an appraisal discussion in a very indirect way, was out of step, together with a momentary lapse in 53.

SUMMARY

We have looked at two interactions, in an attempt to clarify the links between behavior and objectives. The first was an example of an ends and means failure; the second was a success on both counts.

This sort of analysis has shown that it is possible to think of behavior in terms of its in or out of stepness with objectives, provided the objectives are specific enough. The next chapter concentrates attention on objectives, since they are the pivot on which behavior rotates.

One last point before we move on: The case studies we have looked at so far could lead you to conclude that means and ends always go hand in hand, together with a sort of inevitable correlation between the two. Alas, this is not so. It is quite possible to fail to achieve your ends, even though your behavior throughout the interaction was totally compatible with the objective. It is also possible for your objective to be realized quite fortuitously when predominantly out of step behaviors have been used. This is because behavior is only one factor amongst many that determine success or failure. Interactive skill is all about arranging behavior so that we increase the *probability* of being successful. There are no guarantees that it will always work.

4

Working Out Realistic Objectives for Face to Face Encounters

As a subject matter, objectives are undoubtedly a bore. At best, they are a discipline forcing us to specify things clearly and precisely. At worst, they are an uncomfortable threat. I have noticed with some sympathy the lengths people will go to in avoiding the business of defining objectives. Common comments are:

"It isn't possible to set precise objectives in our sort of work, of course. We have to play things largely by ear."

"Objectives don't make any difference to what we do on a day to day basis. Just because we write down an objective it doesn't change anything."

"Objectives? Yes, I've got some somewhere in this drawer. . .I think. . . ."

"Objectives are just a nasty way of pinning people down and depriving them of initiative."

"Objectives spoil our fun. We enjoy 'fire fighting,' reacting to situations, never knowing what is going to happen next. They take the thrill out of spontaneity. They aren't natural."

It is really tragic that objectives, by and large, are so misunderstood and have such a jaded reputation—tragic but inevitable. The process of working out objectives *is* inherently tedious. The discipline of writing objectives down is just that—a discipline. And, when all is said and done, objectives in themselves *don't* change anything. They require *activity*, in the form of plans and actions to bring them to life. Since activity is necessary, with or without objectives, many people conclude that objectives are an optional extra they can happily dispense with.

The *intellectual* case for objectives is, however, strong. It can be argued it is not a question of deciding whether to have objectives or not. There is not an either-or choice. Man is a purposeful animal, and as such he *always* has objectives. The only choice we have is whether to fashion the objectives that are there anyway into a form where they can be articulated.

The skills involved in making objectives conscious and capable of articulation are our primary concern in this chapter. As we saw in Chapter 2, objectives occupy a central role in interactive skills, since they form the vital bridge between situations and behavior itself. Before going on to look at the mechanics of working out objectives, let me put the case for bothering at all.

Research shows that a typical manager spends something like 80 per cent of his time in face to face interaction with people as a legitimate part of his job. Many of them don't *feel* it is legitimate, as revealed when they say things like: "I get into the office early so that I can get on with some *real* work before the interruptions start." Or, "What a day! Non-stop meetings and nothing achieved. I'll have to take all this work home with me." I have an idea that the attitude that interacting is not really working is the key to understanding why acceptance of sloppy, shapeless rambling interactions is so widespread. Paradoxically, it may be precisely *because* our expectations are set so low that we feel interactions are destined to remain this way and are somehow immune to significant improvement. On the whole, I have found managers to be amazed at the notion that interactions, and not just grander, longer-term activities, benefit from having precise objectives. I have stopped managers in mid-interactive flight, as it were, and asked them to tell me what their objectives for the current interaction were. I know of no surer way of reducing them to hesitant "umming and urring!" In my experience, people are much clearer about their "middle distance" objectives, six months and one year hence, than they are about their immediate, here and now ones. Yet 80 per cent of time is absorbed in interactions of one sort or another: big and small ones, formal and informal ones. That is where, day by day, both time and effort go. Taken singly, therefore, each interaction may seem of insufficient consequence to go to the trouble to have conscious objectives and the other accompanying paraphernalia. Taken collectively, however, interactions are where productivity can easily hit an all time low. Accordingly, I believe that if anything *can* be done to improve the quality and productivity of interactions it would be a really significant contribution. Having conscious objectives for interactions is part of the answer. Behaving properly, in accordance with the objectives, is the other part.

WHAT IS AN OBJECTIVE?

Basically, an objective is a prediction about the state of affairs that you wish to exist at some specified time in the future. An objective is always arrived at by making a judgment about how much it is reasonable to achieve in a given period.

The way people make this judgment differs considerably from individual to individual. Some are brave and risk committing themselves to an enormously challenging objective on a flimsy data base. Others are much more cautious. They wait longer before taking the plunge. They assemble as much information about the situation as they can. They hedge their bets by building "either-or" type escape clauses into the objective. The *really* cautious have two favorite ploys for protecting themselves against being wrong in their prediction. One is deliberately to leave the objective hazy and vague so that they have room to maneuver in claiming that subsequent events were in fact predicted accurately. In a group, I often find that when someone says, "Oh come on! We are just playing with semantics. We all know what we mean," it is a sign that the rigors of defining a precise enough objective are proving too demanding. I have watched managers go to the very brink of defining a specific objective only to retreat back into the comfort of fudging the issue.

The other ploy, which some have developed into an accomplished game for survival, is to postpone the setting of the objective until either the eleventh hour before the event the objectives are supposed to predict or, if they are really smart, until *after* the event they are supposed to predict! This is a convenient way of always being right. No matter what happens, you can claim that the outcome was the one you were aiming for!

These and other ploys miss the essence of what objectives are all about: making a sharp, precise prediction of the state of affairs which will exist, if you have been successful, at a specified time in the future.

An objective is a statement articulating the outcome you want from a situation. The statement needs to be as specific and unambiguous as possible. It helps if the expression of the objective contains two elements. First, a nutshell description of the outcome you want. Secondly, some standards of success, so stated that they qualify any ambiguity in the nutshell description and can act, eventually, as practical indicators or measures of your success or failure.

Since, in this book, we are concentrating on face to face interactions, our concern is quite properly going to be with how to set objectives for interactions of various kinds. In fact, the only difference between an objective for an interaction and any other sort of activity is purely one of longevity.

The definition of an objective in the last paragraph is equally applicable whether we are talking about long-term objectives or short-term ones. A satisfactory articulation of intent contains the same basic ingredients.

Being able to distinguish between objectives occupying different time phases is a crucial skill if you are to be clear about the sorts of objectives it is realistic to go for in a thing like an interaction. As everyone knows, interactions have fairly severe limits. The maxim "when all is said and done, far more is said than done" rings very true. Interactions *are*, by their very nature, confined. The accent is usually on agreeing things, planning things, and deciding things— rarely on actually *doing* things. The doing usually comes after, or in between, interactions.

Let us take an example to illustrate this. Suppose you are a manager with a group of staff who, on the whole, are a good bunch—with one exception. Your boss has asked you to take some action about this weak member within the next six months. What action you take is up to you. The man in question is always willing to undertake new work, but somehow it never seems to get done precisely as you have asked or, more importantly, on time. He is always ready with the reasons, many of them very plausible, why it couldn't be done—afterwards!

Two weeks ago, you asked him to prepare an important report for you. The matter was to be treated as urgent, and the report should have been completed and received by you yesterday. It is only because you were hopelessly busy yourself yesterday that you didn't check up on its whereabouts. Now the subordinate has asked to see you to complain about being overloaded with work. You have to find some way of dealing with the immediate problems as well as making some progress in improving his longer-term performance. You can only spare one hour before having to keep another appointment.

That, then, is the situation. The problem is now to decide how much it is desirable and realistic to achieve in the interaction with your subordinate. Without worrying about dotting all the I's and crossing all the T's, here are a few of the choices that face you:

a. To have explored his complaint about being over-worked and convinced him that it was unfounded

b. To have reviewed progress on the missing report and committed him to completion by (a time acceptable to you in the light of the work that remained to be done on it and its urgency)

c. To have appraised his overall performance and produced an action plan aimed at making him more reliable

d. To have improved his performance so that he always gets work done to the standards set and completed on time.

Apart from variations in detail, one of the most significant differences between these four possibilities is in terms of their ambitiousness. The first one doesn't push the issue nearly as far as the second. The second doesn't push it as far as the third, and so on. They represent very different judgments about how far it is realistic to go within the time span of the interaction. This judgment is important because it is fundamental in predisposing the outcome. If you decide to aim for the fourth objective, for example, you will fail—simply because it expresses a level of achievement far in excess of anything that could be accomplished in one interaction. The fourth objective may well be an expression of what you are *ultimately* aiming at, but knowing that isn't likely to leave you much clearer about what to strive to achieve in the immediate interaction.

Then again, if you decide to go for the third objective, you may also fail, simply because one hour is unlikely to be long enough for this level of accomplishment. On the other hand, if you go for the first, you may succeed totally; but that might strike you as "cold comfort," since the first objective pinpoints an inadequate success in the context of the missing report and the subordinate's persistent performance problems.

It is often easier to recognize "wrong" objectives than it is to be definitive about which are "right." What is "right" in part depends on your own skills as a participant in the situation. It *is* possible to say, however, that the objective you set should always be:

   a. *In step* with your analysis of the situation
   b. *Realistic*, in the sense that you judge it is genuinely possible to be successful
   c. *Challenging*, in the sense that being successful isn't a near certainty but will have to be earned.

Just to round off the earlier example, but not to pretend to give the only or "right" answer, here is the objective that I would aim for in my interaction with the subordinate:

   To have produced a plan that he can adhere to to prevent him taking on work that he can't get done on time. I will have been successful if:

   a. The plan is specific enough such that he can run through the "drill" he has to follow without me having to correct him significantly.
   b. He will have suggested more of the content of the plan than I have had to.
   c. He will thank me for having helped to solve his problem.
   d. He will offer to produce the missing report by a time that I consider reasonable in the light of the fact that it is already a day late and is urgent.

THE BENEFITS OF SETTING OBJECTIVES FOR INTERACTIONS

There are really three interrelated benefits to be reaped by having clear, precise objectives when interacting.

First, the objective helps you to be clear about what you have to *do* in a bid to get it to come true. It is amazing to me how few people seem to have made the conceptual leap from objectives to activities. Indeed, many find it difficult to distinguish between the two—more about that in the next section when we look at some of the pitfalls to avoid when setting objectives. Too often, the objective is viewed as a rather troublesome thing that needs minimal maintenance—like updating it now and again. In fact living, as opposed to dead, objectives continually influence all activities that follow in their wake. Decisions and plans need to be made in the light of the objective. For example, the objective helps to shape your behavior. Conscious knowledge of the objective means that you can spot, and even curb, irrelevancies and be better at controlling your behavior so that it contributes to its achievement. Subsequent chapters on planning and shaping behavior will expand on these activities, but always against the backdrop of objectives themselves.

A second benefit in having clear, precise objectives is that it makes it easy to compare the actual outcome with your prediction. This means you can be quite certain about total success, relative success, failure, and so on. This, in turn, means that you are in a better position to learn from experience. During a program I was running recently, this emphasis on consciously monitoring performance and learning from experience became encapsulated in the group's *modus operandi* to such an extent that whenever they "failed" they would chant: "There's no such thing as failure: only opportunities to learn!" Without objectives, you can never quite be sure about how to view the outcome, and this is especially true of interactions. It is so easy to muddle through, sliding from one interaction to the next with no sharp concept of the degree of success you are attaining. And remember that for most of us, something like 80 per cent of our working time can be absorbed in this way.

Finally, the third benefit is that, if you consciously have an objective in mind, it helps you to communicate to others what you want to achieve. Quite clearly, if you yourself aren't too sure of your objective, you aren't in a position to decide whether to reveal it to others or not. Saying what your objectives are in interaction is only possible if they are in a form that makes their articulation possible. I believe that interactions often meander on in their fuzzy way precisely because participants are literally lost for words in describing what they wish to achieve. This leads to all sorts of weird goings-on like, for example, spending a whole interaction discovering, through a sea of innuendos, that the parties involved have substantially different objectives. This discovery need not have been so tortuous if the objectives had been in a communicable form. In fact, differences could have been established within the first 10 minutes. I am not suggesting that explicitly declaring your objectives is any sort of golden rule, but it is surprising how often simply *saying* what your objectives are is entirely compatible with making it as likely as possible that they will be achieved.

There are other benefits in setting objectives, but I hope these three are appealing enough to commend the approach to you.

SOME PITFALLS TO AVOID
WHEN SETTING OBJECTIVES

There are four particular pitfalls to avoid when setting objectives. The first is much more difficult to pinpoint in cold print than the other three, which are much more mechanistic.

The first hazard is to avoid having objectives that only have tenuous links with the situation itself. This is really the in step, out of step concept over again except that this time it relates to the bonding between situations and objectives rather than between objectives and behavior. The pitfall is to pay only cursory attention to the factors that comprise the situation and, consequently to set objectives that do not really fit the circumstances. In practice, the objective should cascade out of your understanding of the situation in a fairly effortless way. The more you have to work at contriving it, the less likely it is to dovetail with the real situation. The acid test is to imagine that someone is going to audit your objective and demand to know how each part relates to the situation. If you can satisfy the auditor that each bit of the objective is in step with the situation, then you have survived the first hazard.

The second hazard is to have overall objectives instead of end of interaction ones. Going into an interaction with objectives like "To make a profit," "To cut the incidence of industrial action by 50 per cent," "To improve Bill's managerial performance" is totally inadequate. These are longer-term, or overall, objectives that cannot possibly be achieved within the life-span of an interaction. Certainly it is of the utmost importance to be aware of the overall objective. For one thing, we need to know it in order to mesh the step-by-step, interaction by interaction, activity by activity objectives in with it. But overall objectives are not adequate in guiding us satisfactorily through interactions that, remember, can take up to 80 per cent of our time. We must have shorter term objectives to guide us through here-and-now happenings like interactions. For example, the problem with having an objective like "To improve Bill's managerial performance" is that it is unlikely to be achieved just by a single interaction with him.

There is more to it than that! To be clear about how much to achieve in an interaction with Bill, we need to backtrack from this expression of an overall objective. Judgments about what it is reasonable to go for by the end of the interaction will vary, but for the sake of this example let us say that the immediate objective could be: "To agree on criteria for judging Bill's performance as a manager." Let us freeze the example there for a minute and return to it when we have considered the third pitfall.

The third hazard when setting objectives is not specifying standards of success. Earlier we defined an objective as: "a statement articulating the outcome you desire from a situation. The statement needs to be as specific and unambiguous as possible. It helps if the objective contains two elements: first, a nutshell description of the outcome you desire, secondly, some standards of success, so stated that they qualify any ambiguity in the nutshell description and can act as practical indicators, or measures of your success or failure."

If we merely have the "nutshell description" as our end-of-interaction objective, we are nearly back to the perils we have just been discussing when having overall objectives as a replacement for more immediate ones. The problem is that we have left ourselves too much room for maneuvering. This may seem an advantage rather than a snag, except that it means we deny ourselves at least two out of the three benefits described on pages 74 to 75. You cannot be sufficiently clear what you have to *do* to accomplish the objective if it is vague. You are also hard put to it (except by rationalizing) to assess the extent of your success or failure.

The answer is to spice up the prediction by including standards of success as an integral part of the objective. Without them, we are just playing at predicting in the same way that a soothsayer might when couching forecasts in such vague terms that whatever happens is bound to compare favorably with it. Specifying standards of success forces us to take the nutshell statement and tighten it up. Standards might be set in some, or all, of the following areas:

a. *The amount of work* that will have been accomplished by the end of the interaction if it is to be judged a success

b. *The quality of work* that will have been done by the end of the interaction

c. *The behavior* that the other person, or persons, will have displayed by the end of the interaction if it is to be judged a success. Including behavioral standards is vital since behavior is the visible aspect. How someone reacts in interaction is a vital indicator to how they are likely to behave after it

    d. *The time* it will have taken to accomplish the end-of-interaction objective.

In order to exemplify these, let us return to the example we started earlier about improving Bill's managerial performance.

    If you remember, we shrunk this overall objective down into the immediate one of having a session with Bill where we would "agree upon the criteria for judging Bill's performance as a manager." Possible standards of success might be:

    a. *For the amount of work:* "We will have produced at least six criteria."

    b. *For the quality of work:* "The criteria will be in writing, and each will be specific enough to make it possible for Bill and me to judge his performance against it without hesitation and interpolation and, in so doing, to reach the same conclusion."

    c. *For behavior:*
"Bill will have spontaneously suggested at least half the criteria"
"Bill will have spontaneously remarked that the session has helped him to be clear about what is involved in being a good manager"
"Bill will volunteer to get the criteria typed out with a copy for me"
"Bill will be able to run through the criteria (in his own words) without leaving any out and without it being necessary for me to 'correct' him because of any difference in understanding between us."

    d. *For time:* "Not more than one hour."

If you feel uncertain about how to articulate standards of this kind, try the exercises towards the end of this chapter on page 81. There are six different situations for which to analyze and set end-of-interaction objectives. You might also look back at the sample objectives we were using as our backdrop in the earlier exercises to do with judging the in or out of step relationship with behavior. The essential point about standards is that the sharper and more precise your definition of success can be, short of becoming hair splitting, the easier it is to shape activities and behavior accordingly.

The final hazard to mention in this section relates back to some earlier points made about the need to distinguish between objectives and activities. In teaching circles, it is the difference between reading a Shakespeare play and what the teacher wants the pupil to get out of reading it. The former is an activity, the latter the objective. Returning to our example, therefore, we could list a number of activities, but their sum total does not amount to the end-of-interaction objective. The objective should be a "snapshot" prediction, capturing the state of affairs we want to exist by the end of the interaction. The activities, on the other hand, are the ongoing plan, or agenda, we shall use to guide us through the interaction. For example, we might list the following activities as part of the plan for our interaction with Bill:

a. To get him to admit that he has some problems in managing properly
b. To establish why he finds it difficult to manage
c. To convince him that having some explicit criteria might help
d. To produce the list of criteria.

This sort of "shopping list" is not an end-of-interaction objective. Contrast it with the objective developed earlier on page 78. Notice that only the last activity in our chronological listing of activities comes close to the objective we set. This underlines the vital fact that the objective should be concerned with defining the end point of the interaction and not be confused with the plan for how to proceed towards that end point.

In conclusion can I say that setting "good" objectives that compare favorably with the definition is not easy, but we have to practice it if we are to qualify for the benefits discussed earlier. The discipline of thinking through objectives to a sufficient level of specificity is rejected by many people as too onerous. In my experience, however, people who *have* trained themselves, quite literally, to *live*-by-objectives have gained a whole new perspective in their lives besides becoming more effective in their people-transactions. Objectives certainly "beef-up" interactions that would otherwise be unrewarding and routine.

People who have had bad experiences with objectives, and there are plenty of casualties, often insist that they should not be bound by specific objectives but should feel free to take up whatever happens to be of interest at the moment. Objectives, they say, confine them to a narrow prescribed route and blind them to alternative, perhaps more appropriate, courses of action. A good objective states an end point that can be achieved in many different ways. *How* we got Bill to join us in agreeing upon six criteria could have been done using a variety of different approaches. Ironically, concentrating on objectives instead of on the "shopping list" agenda leaves us *free* to try new approaches. Rather than hamper creativity, objectives stimulate us to try new and more efficient behavioral approaches. In any case, objectives need not be immutable. New standards can be added and old ones discarded or changed. But it is important to accept that whenever we consciously modify an objective the need to do so is, in itself, an indictment of the judgments we have made in the light of the situation about what it was realistic to attempt. Of course we need to abandon an objective if, as the interaction unfolds, it strikes us as absurd, and replace it with something more reasonable; but this should not happen too frequently. Chopping and changing objectives is likely to make our behavior appear as confusing as not having any objectives at all. The "freedom," or spontaneity, that comes from no objectives, or vague ones, is largely illusory, for it leaves us particularly susceptible to other people's objectives and vulnerable to any familiar routines. Objectives stimulate rather than hamper creativity.

EXERCISES IN SETTING REALISTIC OBJECTIVES FOR FACE TO FACE ENCOUNTERS

Here are six descriptions of different situations. They are only the bare bones, and in each case you will need to make some assumptions in adding flesh to the bones. The idea is to work out what end-of-interaction objective you consider realistic and rigorous enough within the context of each situation. There are no right answers, but, in order to give you a basis of comparison, I have written out my ideas on suitable objectives (they follow immediately after the chapter summary, on page 85). If you do not wish to work your way through all six situations, try your hand at a couple. I recommend that you select the two which have the most similarity with the sort of everyday situations you are used to tackling.

Situation 1: Delegation Problem

One of your subordinates has one real shortcoming: He will not delegate. Whenever there is any semblance of a crisis he goes in and does the job himself. When tackled on this, he claims that his people respect him for being able to do a better job than they can or says that he likes "to keep his hand in." You suspect that his people resent these interventions whenever something is getting really interesting and regard them as a vote of no confidence in their work. Furthermore, you have noticed that this inability or unwillingness to delegate results in your subordinate taking too much on himself. He frequently stays late to "catch up" and increasingly fails to get jobs done by their deadlines. You decide that you have got to tackle this problem and get him to delegate more.

Situation 2: Procrastinating Boss

Your boss is a renowned verbal rambler and procrastinator. You need a decision—urgently.

In 30 minutes, a very good customer prospect is due to arrive to meet you. You have already had a series of meetings and things are looking good. Three days ago you had a session with your boss when you asked if you might make some concession on this prospective customer which you are sure will clinch the deal. You didn't bother him with precise details of the concessions you expect are necessary— you were more interested in getting his blessing in principle with some guidance about how much room for maneuvering you were permitted.

You have already needled him twice since then for a decision. Once he said he was still thinking about it and the second time he was just rushing off to some meeting or other. You are now going to see him to try to get a decision and you predict that he won't have made his mind up and will still be "worrying" about it.

Situation 3: Taking Over New Departments

You have just been appointed departmental manager of a newly formed department. Your department contains three branches. One of them you know intimately, having run it yourself for three years. It is now run by one of the people in that branch with whom you worked closely and successfully. The two other branches are a service branch which you never used or thought much of before and a branch selling a fairly technical product direct to the customer. You are not familiar with either the product or with operating in a direct-to-the-customer environment.

The branch from which you came is in many ways more advanced in its work than the other two. Its staff are on average higher paid, for instance, and its "specialness" has been known to cause resentment.

You only know the two branch managers to say "hello" to, and you are anxious to get off to a good start with them both. So you have arranged to meet them, one at a time, for an initial "getting to know each other" couple of hours.

Situation 4: The Ideas Man

You have a colleague with whom you have worked on a number of projects in the past. You know him as a guy who is always coming up with ideas, some good, some mediocre, and some appalling. He seems to go for quantity of ideas and to let other people worry about quality. This hasn't earned him a very good reputation, since the work "culture" seems to put a higher premium on good ideas rather than on a lot of ideas.

He has sent you a draft of a new idea he has had, worked out in enormous detail. He wants to come and discuss it with you as someone whose views are important to him, not as someone who will be involved in any future implementation of the idea. Unfortunately, you think the idea is completely unworkable in its present form, although you recognize there is a germ of value in it.

He respects your opinion. You hope to steer him away from making a fool of himself without losing his respect.

Situation 5: Activity Diaries

You have to brief a group of your subordinates on the part they are to play in a nationwide exercise to obtain information about how they spend their working time. It involves them in keeping an activity diary each day for a month: a laborious and unrewarding task.

You are experiencing some irritation, as it is not long since a similar request was made. No one, including you, heard the outcome of the previous study, and several doubted its necessity.

You have put it on the agenda of a meeting you are due to have with all your subordinates, and you wonder how you can break the news of this imposed chore and get enough commitment from them at the same time.

Situation 6: Salesman's Expenses

You are an area sales manager appointed just six months ago. One of your best salesmen, with an extremely good record, is inclined to "pad" quite a lot of his expenses. He is on a basic salary plus bonus system and his earnings are substantial. You were shocked by the level of these expenses from the start but approved the claim for the first two months without querying anything with him. You knew this was sheer cowardice at the time, but hoped the situation would resolve itself. It didn't, and so in the third month you spoke to him about the high level of his expenses. He was sullen but agreed to watch them. Since then, you haven't been able to detect the slightest change.

You are about to meet him to take up the matter of expenses for the second time. You expect him to feel that his good sales record more than justifies the level of expenses and to see you as being unnecessarily petty in raising the matter again.

SUMMARY

The chapter has concentrated on objectives. It started by admitting to their unpopularity, but, despite this, went on to look at the benefits they bring and what was involved in making objectives conscious and capable of articulation.

A number of reasons were advanced in support of objectives. We saw that even though each single interaction might seem of little consequence, collectively they can consume as much as 80 per cent of a manager's working time. Accordingly, three benefits were identified for having conscious objectives: that they help us to be clear about what activities are necessary; that they make it easy to compare the actual outcome with the prediction; and, finally, that if objectives are conscious then, if need be, they are declarable to others.

An objective was defined. In general terms, objectives were described as predictions of the state of affairs that we wished to exist at some time in the future. More precisely, an objective was defined as a specific and unambiguous statement, articulating the outcome desired from a situation with standards pinpointing the acceptable level of success.

A number of common confusions it is easy to fall prey to were also examined. In summary, these were: the perils of mistaking plans and activities for objectives; and, finally, the hazard of leaving an objective vague and hazy without standards that describe the level of success required.

The chapter ended with the invitation to try your hand at setting realistic, end-of-interaction objectives for all, or some, of six descriptions of different situations. My own "solutions" are given below.

SAMPLE OBJECTIVES FOR THE SIX SITUATIONS GIVEN ON PAGES 81 TO 83

I must reiterate that these are not the only satisfactory "solutions" to the situations given earlier. You could have substantially different ideas on suitable objectives and still be as "right" as the ones given below. This is because, as we have seen throughout Chapter 4, setting objectives is a peculiarly personal affair. Judgments about what is realistic, about what is in step with the situation, and, for that matter, about what is unambiguous, inevitably vary from person to person.

That understood, here are my thoughts on suitable objectives for each situation.

Situation 1: Delegation Problem

To have produced a plan with X which sorts out which of the jobs he is currently doing himself can be given to someone else and identifies that person. The plan will also include what he can do to stop intervening in a crisis.

I shall have been successful if:

a. The plan we have produced includes details on what, how, who, where, and when.
b. The plan has allocated a minimum of four jobs which X is currently doing himself to someone else.
c. X has subscribed to the plan and said that it has been a helpful session. Also, that he is going to put the plan into action.
d. X has himself suggested that sometime in the future there should be a further meeting to review the success of the plan and to make another one if necessary.
e. This has been achieved within two hours.

Situation 2: Procrastinating Boss

To have got him to agree to all the concessions I am likely to need within 20 minutes.
I shall have been successful if I achieve this in such a way that:

a. He will have shown no sign of resentment at being "nagged" or pushed into a decision.
b. He will have shared the contribution rate with me to a maximum of 50 per cent.
c. He will have said that he is quite happy with the concession arrangement.

Situation 3: Taking Over New Departments

(For both branch managers in turn.) To have produced a list of items for our next working meeting together.
I shall have been successful if:

a. The list has at least six items on it, all of which genuinely require both of us.
b. It has been produced in not less than one and not more than two hours.
c. He has contributed a minimum of half the items listed himself.

d. The date and time for the next meeting will have been agreed between us before we break up.
e. He has said that he looks forward to the next meeting in such a way that I'm inclined to think he really means it.

Situation 4: The Ideas Man

To have got him to agree to a substantial rethinking of his idea in order to make it workable.
I shall have been successful if:

a. He has accepted that at least half of the difficulties I raise in relation to his idea *are* genuine snags.
b. He has said in his own words without any prompting from me, that he now sees that the "culture" is geared to appreciate the quality as well as the quantity of ideas.
c. He has told me that I've done him a big favor and asked if he might return at some later stage to check out the modified idea with me.
d. This has been achieved in a maximum of one hour.

Situation 5: Activity Diaries

To have got them to identify the benefits *to us* of keeping activity diaries and to have planned how to cash in on some of those benefits.
I shall have been successful if:

a. A minimum of half my subordinates have said that they agree that the benefits we have identified *are real* benefits.
b. Our plans do not cut across or interfere with the data head office needs from the activity records.
c. The plan we have produced includes the usual elements of how, who, where, and when.
d. Our plan will not be so ambitious that putting it into action is likely to interfere with work, other than the

normal interruption caused by keeping an activity record accurately for one month.

e. I have judged that the plan, when put into action, will
succeed in achieving 50 per cent of the identified
benefits.

f. This has been achieved in a maximum of two hours.

Situation 6: Salesman's Expenses

To have got him to set a new standard of performance
for himself which controls his level of expenses.
I shall have been successful if:

a. He has set the standard, not me.

b. The standard he has set accords with my own ideas on
a suitable level of expenses.

c. He has agreed that the standard will be binding for
the next three months, after which he will review it.

d. He has said that he now sees that a "good" salesman is
not just someone who brings in sales, but someone
who has a feel for his revenue to cost ratio.

e. This has been achieved within a maximum of one and
a half hours.

5

How to Analyze Behavior

It is time to let objectives slip into the background and to focus the limelight on behavior once again. In the opening chapters, we defined behavior as everything we do which is overt and therefore immediately visible. One of the benefits of this definition was that it meant that any aspect of behavior could be observed and monitored in a straightforward way, without the need for sweeping interpretations. In this chapter, the concept is developed in much more detail, together with some practical exercises aimed at improving your skill in doing a blow by blow analysis.

So far, we have looked at behavior in a rough and ready sort of way. Deciding whether a behavior is in or out of step with objectives requires a *global* judgment. We now need to analyze behavior much more carefully by breaking it down into smaller particles in order to understand the effects brought about by different behaviors.

The idea of breaking behavior down into "bits" and studying the interplay between them is not new. Indeed, worthwhile breakthroughs in the natural sciences usually have come as a result of painstaking attention to detail. The most obvious examples are to be found with studies into animal behavior. In fact, if you read accounts of animal experiments, the attention to detail may strike you as bordering on the neurotic. Drops of saliva are carefully counted, the rate of working levers and tread wheels is monitored on a 24 hour basis, the exact positions ducks take up on a lake is plotted on a grid by an army of observers, every hesitation a rat makes in finding its way through a maze is captured on film. In respectable experimental designs, environmental variables are also controlled in minute detail so that changes in the behavior can be associated with certain environmental conditions, not to others.

The same attention to detail rarely extends to human behavior. Frequently this is because problems of human behavior—delinquency and violence, for example—are so pressing that public opinion has not the patience to let researchers start at square one. This sort of political and social pressure has meant that psychology has had a tough first 70 years trying to establish its credibility as a respectable science. Behavioral problems are on such a massive scale that the contrast between them, with all their attendant urgency, and the plodding, micro, and often dispassionate research by psychologists, seems intolerable. People demand to know "What have experiments where subjects learn a list of nonsense syllables to do with increasing illiteracy?" "What have those silly questions in intelligence tests to do with being successful in life?" "What have interpretations of 'ink blots' to do with vandalism?"

There are similar risks of incurring your indignation when I suggest that one of the basic skills in interacting competently is that of analyzing behavior in some detail. We need some technique that breaks behavior down into relevant but smaller particles than most of us are used to in everyday life. The technique I recommend was first used as a research tool, but particularly in the last few years, has enjoyed a revival as a method with practical pay-offs for us all.

In essence, behavior analysis is the process of breaking down behavior into fairly specific "bits" and labeling the bits with what are called behavior categories. Since by definition any aspect of overt behavior can be directly observed, it follows that all behaviors *can* be categorized. If we thought it useful, we could monitor eyelid movements, eyebrow twitches, finger strumming, and head nodding and shaking. Again, making the important proviso *if we thought it useful*, we could monitor all sorts of verbal behaviors, such as how frequently someone said "you know," how often someone swore, how often someone's Rs sounded like Ws. But we are not going to be particularly concerned with any of these in this book and they are only used to reinforce the following points: that *any* behaviors are amenable to this analytical process; that behavior analysis deals in relatively small "bits"; and that choices about which "bits" it is relevant to attend to are vitally important both from the point of view of practical expediency and of credibility for the technique. Monitoring eyebrow movements would neither be very useful nor credible in most managerial situations.

With behavior analysis techniques, we can take descriptions of behavior at a more general "styles" level and break them down into their constituent parts. Examples of "styles" level descriptions are:

"He is a very *demanding* boss."
"He seems so *aggressive*."
"He is a good *leader*."
"He strikes me as utterly *genuine*."
"He is rather *autocratic*."
"He is very *participative*."
"He is *determined*."
"He is an *entrepreneur*."

Descriptions like these are used hundreds of times each day. They are useful in everyday conversation, but too ambiguous for planning purposes. The training manager, for example, wants to break down these styles into behavioral specifications so that he can design behavior change programs. The personnel manager, with the headache of advising on selection techniques, wants to translate vague notions about having business acumen or being an entrepreneur into behavioral skills that can be assessed in the selection process. And, much more important, *all of us* need to know how to arrange our behavior so that we *are* determined, a good leader, genuine, and so on. Time and time again I have been on behavioral science programs where the invitation to experiment with different ways of behaving has been extended. The problem is how? What do I have to *do* to pull my behavior out of its well-worn ruts and try "unnatural" alien behaviors? The invitation to change or experiment sounds plausible enough. Accepting it involves the skills of consciously arranging an outward display of certain behaviors and controlling the occurrence of others: the very *same* skills that we need if we are to be able to adjust behavior so that it is in step with different objectives.

The "secret," inasmuch as there is one, is to break style-level descriptions down into smaller behavioral bits. Our behavior plan can then be built around the "bits" instead of depending on vague intentions. Intentions are infamous for getting put into action less frequently than plans simply because intentions leave a yawning gap that only plans can bridge. *Intending* to get up early and do two hours work before breakfast is less likely to happen than if we plan to do it. Planning involves a series of action steps, such as going to bed earlier than usual and setting the alarm or alarms. Planning behavior is the subject of a later chapter. Our immediate concern in this one is to establish a technique for analyzing behavior.

Styles, then, are, in effect, *conclusions* we reach about the way others operate. The conclusions are based on observations of smaller behavioral "bits." Here are some examples.

Participative breaks down into the following behavioral "bits": Lots of seeking behaviors where the person explicitly asks for opinions, ideas, suggestions, and proposals from others. The participative person also asks lots of questions of clarification and even puts his own ideas in the form of questions to people. When reacting to whatever suggestions and proposals are forthcoming, the participative person mainly supports and develops the ideas rather than squashing them.

Autocratic breaks down into the following behavioral "bits": Lots of telling and, proportionally, little asking. The autocratic person does not ask others for their ideas. He generates lots of proposals and they rarely seem tentative or "up for discussion" but are more in the form of instructions or commands. Autocrats interrupt others when they are talking. Overall, the autocratic person also mainly disagrees with, or points out, the snags in other people's suggestions

Determined breaks down into the following behavioral "bits": Answers questions without hesitation. Doesn't "um and ur." Speaks fast. Looks people straight in the eye.

Genuine breaks down into the following behavioral "bits": Expresses feelings more than using factual-type information. Messages given by verbal behavior do not differ from messages given by accompanying nonverbal behavior (i.e., you don't greet someone by saying "I've been longing to meet you" with your head down, rummaging through a pile of papers!).

Clearly, any style-level description is amenable to this sort of analysis by reversing the synthetic process that we all use to reach communicable conclusions about people. The danger in doing this is to break down styles into such fragmented "bits" that synthesizing is impaired and we are unable to relate the "bits" to the various styles. If I broke a cup into six pieces, for example, and displayed them, you could easily synthesize from the pieces to a whole cup. If, however, I pulverized the cup and showed you a heap of powder, it is most unlikely that you could conclude it was once a cup. We must be careful not to pulverize behavior styles. The whole point of a behavior analysis technique is to become clearer about what is going on during a transaction. To do this, we need analysis *and* synthesis.

BENEFITS OF BEHAVIOR ANALYSIS

There are four interrelated benefits to be gained with a behavior analysis approach. First, the behavior categories give us a "language" for describing what is happening, at a behavioral level, during interactions between people. The specificity of the language helps in making "discoveries" about the importance of certain behaviors that might be missed at a more general descriptive level.

Secondly, the behavior categories give us a practical means of consciously monitoring our own as well as other people's behavior whenever we want to. Thirdly, the same behavior categories can "double" as a shorthand when thinking about how best to behave in the light of a particular situation and desired objective. Accordingly, the behavior categories make it possible to plan and to control behavior. Behavior planning will be covered in Chapter 8. The final benefit is that behavior analysis helps us to understand how to "shape" other people's behavior in response to our own. Behavior shaping will be explored in Chapter 7.

INTRODUCTORY EXERCISE
IN BEHAVIORAL ANALYSIS

For the remainder of this chapter, we shall concentrate on the first two benefits. Perhaps the best way to do this is to use a short transcript of people in interaction once again. Initially, all you need do is read it through to get a general impression of what is happening and how the participants are behaving.

This is a transcript of part of a meeting between five managers.

    1. FRANK   All right, gentlemen, let's make a start.

    2. PETER   Before we begin on the items listed on this agenda, could I raise another matter?

3. FRANK   I find it hard to imagine what can be so urgent that it isn't already on the agenda or, alternatively, can't wait until Any Other Business.

4. PETER   My reason for bringing it up now was that I hoped my suggestion would have an immediate payoff; whereas if I held it until. . .

5. FRANK   . . .All right. Let's hear your suggestion and *then* decide whether to deal with it right away or put it in somewhere else.

6. TONY   Good idea, Frank.

7. BILL   I can see we are going to finish late again.

8. PETER   Oh, I don't think this will take long. I just want to suggest that since the number of items on the agendas for these meetings increases each time, and that since I have noticed that a good number of items don't concern us all, that we should work out some sort of criterion for deciding whether an item gets onto the agenda or not.

9. FRANK   Criterion? What do you mean?

10. PETER   Well, how about something like "an item qualifies for the agenda if it actively involves at least four of us?"

11. BILL   Oh great, just great! I can see we will spend all our time arguing about what "actively involves" means!

12. TONY   Yes, that would be a difficulty.

13. FRANK   I'm not sure this is worth pursuing; we have a heavy agenda ahead.

14. MIKE   Suppose we sort out what we mean by "actively involves" right now?

15. FRANK   You started this, Peter. Have you got a suggestion?

16. PETER   Have you got a proposal, Mike?

17. MIKE   I suggest that an item will actively involve four of us *if*, throughout the time it is discussed, four of us are able and willing to contribute about equally.

18. BILL   That means that items requiring all of us to

take action *after* the meeting but that don't necessarily require an involved discussion *during* the meeting won't get on the agenda.

19. TONY   Yes, that's right.

20. PETER   All right then, have *two* criteria! The first is Mike's one about everyone being involved in the discussion. And the second one can cope with Bill's point. We could say that an item will "actively involve" four or more of us if, as a result of the item, we are involved in some form of implementation or action after the meeting.

21. BILL   This is getting more like a law convention every minute!

22. FRANK   Gentlemen, we are in danger of never getting this meeting started.

23. MIKE   Just one more thing before we start. Peter's idea will help us to whittle down the number of items on the agenda but won't necessarily be a guarantee that we finish meetings on time. So I suggest that we also apportion a certain amount of time to each item which survives the criteria test.

24. PETER   But you never really know how long you are going to need for an item.

25. BILL   You can say that again. If we had known how long it was going to take to discuss your suggestion. . .

26. FRANK   . . .Well, let's get started now.

27. MIKE   Hang on. Have we agreed on anything or not? Are you suggesting we go ahead and try out these ideas in this current meeting?

28. TONY   I'd be happy to give them a trial run—yes.

29. PETER   The timetable idea isn't going to work, though.

30. FRANK   Look, just let me check that I've got all this. The suggestion is that we start our meetings by going down the agenda to check whether each item will involve four or more of us. And that we then agree on a time limit for each item?

31. MIKE Yes, and another thought occurs to me. Shall we agree that the author of an item which gets scrapped is responsible for finding alternative ways of dealing with it?

32. FRANK And do we have an agenda prepared beforehand in future? Or shall we each come to the meeting with items and start by putting them up for the criterion test? Surely that would be best, on reflection?

33. MIKE Yes, I think so. Now that we have some criteria to apply, let's kick off future meetings by preparing a communally agreed upon agenda. . .

34. PETER I am worried about that. I wasn't thinking of doing away with the advance agenda when I made my suggestion.

35. BILL I can see that all this will take up more time than it will save.

36. MIKE So let's put an overall time limit on the agenda-setting activities: 15 per cent of the total time for the meeting wouldn't seem excessive.

37. TONY Yes, I'll go along with that if you agree, Mr. Chairman?

38. FRANK It isn't a question of whether or not I agree, it seems.

39. PETER I suggest we try this now and for the next couple of meetings, and that we then review the procedure to see if it has been successful.

40. FRANK. Successful? That's rather a difficult concept to apply to things like meetings.

41. MIKE Well, taking Peter's idea a bit further, we could agree that success in this context is that we finish this and the next two meetings not more than 10 minutes over time; that we find our contribution rates to be more even. . .and that we can all genuinely rate the meetings to have improved in relevance and usefulness to each of us.

42. FRANK Okay! Now let's go ahead and apply this procedure to our current agenda.

What did you conclude about the behavior of the participants? Did you get a feel for who was most effective and who least effective? If so, what criteria did you apply in making the judgments? I have tried this particular transcript out on a number of people, and these are typical comments: that Tony was just a yes-man: that Bill was negative and uncooperative: that Frank was a weak, ineffective chairman: that Peter was very constructive and came up with the original idea: that Mike was Peter's main ally and helped him get his suggestion adoped.

Notice how these "gut-feel" reactions are drawn from judgments about two different things. One is the *content* of what is being said and the other is the *behavior* used to express it. To say that Peter's idea was a good or bad one is to make a value judgment about the quality of the idea itself. To debate whether Peter was persuasive or not is to comment on the manner in which he put his idea across to the others. Now, of course, we need to make both sorts of judgments. The quality of people's contributions is clearly enormously important. There would be little merit in having people behaving impeccably, if, in doing so, they produced inadequate ideas. Conversely, it is wasteful to have splendid ideas that don't get taken up because the behavior puts everyone off. We need effective ideas *and* effective behavior, in parallel, the one facilitating the other.

Notice also how these first-feel reactions plunge into making value judgments. We quickly decide what is good and what is bad. We make polarizations between negative and positive, destructive and constructive, relevant and irrelevant, effective and ineffective. These are arrived at in a fairly unthinking way by using our central processor to label events according to our previously learned attitudes. To make judgments about other people's behavior in this way is fine, providing we are not too slap-happy. The subtleties of human behavior are such that we are likely to be wrong at least as often as we are right unless we become more skilled at monitoring behavior in more detail.

One system for deciding who is effective and who

ineffective is to apply the in step, out of step criterion we were practicing earlier (Chapter 3). But suppose we want to enhance this system by going further and pinpointing which sorts of behavior are *most appropriate* in securing an objective? We need some technique for discriminating between different behaviors more precisely than the in step, out of step criterion allows. This is where behavior categories come in.

BEHAVIOR CATEGORIES

The actual behavior categories employed can vary in detail, providing they meet the following general critieria:

a. The categories must be relatively simple, mutually exclusive units of behavior
b. They must be capable of identification by observers with high reliability
c. They must be behavioral or, in other words, must categorize overt behavior without the need for beneath-the-behavioral-surface interpretations
d. They must be meaningful to the individuals who will use them
e. They must have a relationship with the outcomes of the situations in which they are used
f. Finally, they must refer to behavior that can change or is capable of modification.

For our immediate purposes, I propose to introduce a mere nine categories. They are, of course, inadequate in giving *complete* coverage. They have been chosen from a list of 50 or so because they cope with the run of the mill verbal behaviors that occur in different transactions. Incidentally, there is also considerable practical merit in only having nine behavior categories. They are much easier to remember than a longer list. The easier they are to remember, the more likely it is that we can use them when monitoring live behavior and when thinking about which behaviors are most appropriate in different circumstances.

Here are the nine categories, together with some guideline definitions:

Seeking proposals/suggestions. Used whenever someone invites others to contribute ideas, suggestions or proposals. Typical examples are "Has anyone got any ideas on this one?" "Peter, have you any suggestions?" and the like.

Proposing. This category is used to cover contributions which contain a possible course of action, provided (and this is in contrast to the next category) it is put as a statement, announcement or instruction. Examples are "I propose that we do so and so," "We will do the following," "I've got an idea! Let us do so and so," "I suggest that you do so and so."

Suggesting. Still used to cover contributions which contain possible courses of action, but this time they are expressed as a question. Examples are "Shall we do so and so?"; "How about doing so and so?"; "Should we do this or that?"

Building. Still basically a contribution that contains a possible course of action and therefore similar to the proposing and suggesting categories. Building is, however, a special kind of proposing or suggesting in that it is used whenever someone adds to, or develops, someone else's idea, suggestion, or proposal. Meaningful examples are hard to give out of context, but suppose someone put the suggestion: "Suppose we travel to the meeting together in the same car?" And someone else then said: "Yes, and if we picked up Ted en route we could prime him for the meeting too." That would be an example of building. The original course of action has been enhanced by the building behavior.

Disagreeing. The category used to cover all the various ways in which people disagree. Obvious examples are "I disagree," "No, I'm sorry I can't agree with that because. . . ." The category covers flat disagreements as well as those where some reasons or explanation for the disagreement are given.

Supporting. Covers all the various ways of agreeing or giving backing to others' contributions. The most obvious ways of doing this are to say things like "I agree," "Yes, I support your idea." More obscure ways of supporting are more verbose, when, for example, someone backs someone else's suggestion by explaining its merits but not actually adding to the suggestion in any way.

Difficulty stating. The category used to cover contributions where someone points out the snags, problems, and difficulties they see in relation to someone else's contribution. Difficulty stating contributions do not actually contain a disagreement. Classic examples are "The snag with that would be. . ." "We wouldn't be able to do that because. . ." "The problem with that is. . ." This category is used to cover difficulty stating in relation to the content of what others have said as well as difficulty stating about the context of the interaction. So remarks like "This is an absolute shambles. We aren't getting anywhere," "We are running out of time again," "I can't understand a word you are saying" are all included in this difficulty stating category.

Seeking clarification. The category used whenever someone asks for a recap or checks whether he has understood it as it was intended. Examples are "Do you mean so and so?" "Just let me check that I've understood what you've said. Your idea is that we do so and so?" "So you think it would be possible to do so and so?"

Other behavior. The ninth category is used to cover all instances of behavior which do not fit against the eight categories introduced above. In the main, these are:

> Giving clarification and explaining
>
> Summarizing
>
> Checking on the level of agreement
>
> Seeking information (as opposed to suggestions or proposals)
>
> Giving information

In addition, the ninth category can be used to cover any other bits and pieces such as jokes and pure asides.

Those, then, are the categories advocated for initial use. As you become used to thinking in terms of these, you can add some extra ones to give wider coverage and more precision. It is clearly more useful to open up "other behavior," for example, into the five subcategories rather than leave them clustered together in one category. In special instances, other categories may be required to highlight certain behavioral aspects more. In spelling situations, for example, categories such as "initial greeting," "benefit statement," "proof statement," "overcoming objections," "close statement" are often employed. In interviewing situations, categories such as "open-ended questions" and "closed questions" are useful. Such changes in emphasis are entirely appropriate and to be expected, provided the behavior categories used meet the six criteria listed earlier.

Now we are ready to use the categories to describe the behavior of the participants in the transcript. You might like to turn back to it on pages 96 to 99 and note down the category into which you feel each contribution falls. Where you notice that the speaker has employed more than one category in his contribution, categorize it by saying to yourself: "If I were going to speak next, which bit of his behavior would I react to?" This is simply a way of sorting out which part of his contribution you perceived as the most influential.

Here are my categorizations for the transcript.

(1)	Frank	Proposing
(2)	Peter	Suggesting
(3)	Frank	Difficulty stating
(4)	Peter	Other behavior (explaining)
(5)	Frank	Proposing
(6)	Tony	Supporting
(7)	Bill	Difficulty stating
(8)	Peter	Proposing
(9)	Frank	Seeking clarification
(10)	Peter	Suggesting
(11)	Bill	Difficulty stating
(12)	Tony	Supporting
(13)	Frank	Difficulty stating

(14) Mike   Suggesting
(15) Frank   Seeking suggestion/proposal
(16) Peter   Seeking suggestion/proposal
(17) Mike   Building (on Peter in 10)
(18) Bill   Difficulty stating
(19) Tony   Supporting
(20) Peter   Building (on Mike in 17)
(21) Bill   Difficulty stating
(22) Frank   Difficulty stating
(23) Mike   It is not too clear whether this is a fresh proposal or a build on Peter in 20 and/or 10.
(24) Peter   Difficulty stating
(25) Bill   Probably difficulty stating, but he gets cut off prematurely so safer to put it in other behavior
(26) Frank   Proposing
(27) Mike   Seeking clarification
(28) Tony   A vague behavior, not too clear whether this is other behavior (giving clarification) or supporting
(29) Peter   Difficulty stating
(30) Frank   Seeking clarification
(31) Mike   Suggesting
(32) Frank   Suggesting
(33) Mike   Supporting
(34) Peter   Difficulty stating
(35) Bill   Difficulty stating
(36) Mike   Proposing
(37) Tony   Again a vague behavior where the categorization depends on which part you chose to regard as the most influential. The first part is supporting. The second part is other behavior (checking on level of agreement).
(38) Frank   Either other behavior or you may perceive it as difficulty stating but it is a bit obscure
(39) Peter   Proposing
(40) Frank   Difficulty stating

(41) Mike   Building (on Peter in 39)
(42) Frank Proposing

How do the categories help? Are they an aid in making "discoveries" about the importance of certain behaviors that might be missed at a more general descriptive level? Are they an advance on the in step, out of step analysis we tried earlier in the book?

Obviously I am biased! My answers to these questions are an unashamed "yes." But let us return to the characters in the transcript and see if I can convince you that the language of the categories helps us to be clearer about the effectiveness of their interaction. Here is my analysis of each participant in turn:

Frank
It looks as though his objective for this part of the discussion was to curtail it and get on with the "proper" meeting for which they had in fact assembled. Using this as a backdrop, his in step, out of step balance sheet looks like this:

IN STEP	OUT OF STEP
(1) Proposing	(9) Seeking clarification
(3) Difficulty stating	(15) Seeking suggestion
(5) Proposing	(30) Seeking clarification
(13) Difficulty stating	(32) Suggesting
(22) Difficulty stating	(38) Other behavior
(26) Proposing	(40) Difficulty stating
(42) Proposing	
TOTAL 7	6

This is a dodgy overall performance with in step, out of step behaviors practically neck and neck. But now let us use the behavior categories to scrutinize his in step behavior more closely to see if they were as appropriate as possible in the light of his objective (or, more correctly, in the light of the objective that we *imagine* has propelled him through the conversation. We are left wondering, since he nowhere makes it absolutely explicit). Look at Frank in 3, for example. If his objective was to curtail "interruptions" and get on with the "proper" meeting, why merely difficulty state? A more appropriate behavior would have been to go the whole way and disagree. If he had said something like "No, sorry Peter, but I want to move straight on to the agenda items," it is more likely that the issue would have been nipped in the bud and postponed until Any Other Business. It isn't *guaranteed* that this would have worked, but it would certainly have increased the probability, and that is the best that Frank could be expected to do.

Once Frank had greased his own slippery slope, he proceeded to slide down it. In 5, for example, he made a decision that was more in step than out of step with his objective, even though it effectively gave Peter the permission he was seeking to put his proposition now rather than in Any Other Business; 9 was an incredible out of step behavior for Frank. He sought clarification, which of course opened the issue up rather than closing it down. What is more, in doing so, Frank failed to abide by the decision he announced in 5. A feeble attempt at recovery in 13 with a difficulty state which failed and back to being out of step in 15 again, this time opening up the issue by seeking a suggestion; 22 is yet another example of a behavior by Frank aimed at achieving his objective, but, as in the earlier examples (3 and 13), it is a difficulty state and not, in the circumstances, nearly potent enough to make it likely that he would succeed.

Frank failed to achieve his objective, and he deserved to fail, since analysis of his behavior pinpoints precisely how he lost control. If he had been more conscious of his objective, more skilled at monitoring behavior and arranging his own so that it was appropriate, the story might have been different.

Peter
His objective was rather more transparent than Frank's. We can't be sure of his success standards, but,

broadly, his objective must have been to have got his colleagues to adopt his agenda-setting routine in such a way that they would have applied it to the current meeting and agreed to try it at future ones. With this as the backdrop, his in step, out of step performance was:

IN STEP	OUT OF STEP
(2) Suggesting	(24) Difficulty stating
(4) Explaining	(29) Difficulty stating
(8) Proposing	(34) Difficulty stating
(10) Suggesting	
(16) Seeking proposal	
(20) Building	
(39) Proposing	
TOTAL 7	**3**

This was a good overall performance that leads to Peter being largely successful in achieving his objective; 10, 16 and 20 are particularly skillful contributions: 10 because it would have been so easy to reply to Frank in 9 by giving clarification and, whilst to have done so would still have been in step, it certainly would not have been as potent and appropriate as going ahead with a suggestion: 16 because he explicitly invited Mike to put a suggestion or proposal knowing that it was "safe" to do so in the light of what Mike had already said in 14: 20 because having brought Mike in, he proceeded to build on what he had proposed *and* overcame Bill's difficulty at the same time.

Peter's behavior slipped only when he difficulty stated three times about Mike's proposal in 23. In part, this was Mike's "fault" since our analysis left us in doubt about whether Mike was building on Peter's earlier suggestions or producing an essentially new proposal. If Mike had managed to say 23 in such a way that Peter had perceived it as building, then the difficulties might never have emerged as a reaction. Peter recovered his behavior and was entirely back in step by the time he put his proposal in 39.

Bill

It is not too difficult to guess that Bill's objective must have been on the lines of opposing the suggested changes of procedure in such a way that the meeting finishes on time. It is always possible that he had a more obscure objective. You could argue, for example, that he was supporting Peter's ideas for procedural changes by playing devil's advocate! If so, his colleagues could be forgiven for not realizing it. Alternatively, Bill could have been "drifting" through this part of the meeting with no objective. If so, it is a shame that he didn't say less. Interactions might often be much more effective if people were built so that they automatically cut off and their behavior was frozen whilst they had no conscious, articulatable objective. Rather like the children's game of musical statues: the music stops and you freeze—you can only move again when it restarts. No objective: no behavior.

If we assume that Bill's objective was to oppose, his in step, out of step performance was:

IN STEP	OUT OF STEP
	(7) Difficulty stating
	(11) Difficulty stating
	(18) Difficulty stating
	(21) Difficulty stating
	(25) Other behavior
	(35) Difficulty stating
TOTAL 0	**6**

At least he was consistently out of step! Why was this? At first sight, you may have concluded that Bill was opposing fairly effectively. The evidence that he was not is overwhelming.

First, he failed to achieve his objective. Secondly, all his behaviors were out of step with his own objective. Thirdly, the behavior he employed was singularly inappropriate. Indeed, if you examine the effect that his difficulty stating had on the course of the meeting, the irony is that it succeeded in achieving the reverse of Bill's objective. His difficulties actually helped to prolong the meeting and/or to get Peter's idea enhanced. Look at the effect of Bill in 18, for example. It led, more or less directly, to Peter's build in 20. Bill's stated difficulty in 35 had much the same effect, stimulating Mike's proposal in 36. It is true that some of his difficulty stating nearly won useful allies. Bill in 11, for example, was supported by Tony, and encouraged Frank to difficulty state himself in 13. But it was easily counteracted by Mike in 14. Bill seemed to have the same effect on Frank in 21/22 and in 25/26. Bill would have been more likely to succeed if he had either disagreed or put some counter suggestions or proposals. He may have thought he had done his best to oppose, but behavior analysis shows he was using inappropriate behaviors.

Mike
His objective by the time he speaks in 14 seemed to be to have developed Peter's basic idea in such a way that it became an acceptable, workable proposition. His behavior was never out of step with this objective.

IN STEP	OUT OF STEP
(14) Suggesting	
(17) Building	
(23) Proposing/Building?	
(27) Seeking clarification	
(31) Suggesting	
(33) Supporting	
(36) Proposing	
(41) Building	
TOTAL 8	0

An impeccable performance! He uses in step, entirely appropriate behaviors and achieves his objective. The only slight question is whether in 23 he was producing a new idea or an extension of one of Peter's. We discussed the effect this confusion seemed to have earlier, when reviewing Peter's behavior.

Tony

I suspect he didn't have any objective for the part of the discussion under consideration. Some claim that his objective was to keep everyone happy and be popular. I doubt it, however. He definitely came close to taking sides occasionally and, in any case, if he wanted to achieve this objective, he would have had to participate more and use some additional behavior beyond supporting.

Since Tony had no objective, we have no backdrop against which to judge the appropriateness of his behavior unless we have a try at working out what the communal objective for the discussion was and view his behavior against that. As we know, there was never any attempt at producing an explicit, group-agreed objective. This is why we have had to use personal or individual objectives exclusively as our backdrop. After the initial skirmish about when Peter would be allowed to state his idea, the objective of the discussion seems to have been to have decided whether to adopt a change in procedure or not and, if so, to have agreed upon the details of a workable change.

If we view Tony's behavior against this objective, his five contributions are in step, but closer analysis reveals that his behavior was not as appropriate as it could have been. In fact, it is nearly true to say that if Tony were removed from the transcript, nothing that any other participants had to say would need modification. This certainly means that his behavior failed to make any impact on the behavior of his colleagues. Accordingly, I conclude that he was coasting through this phase of the meeting with no commitment to any objective.

I hope this analysis has shown how the language of behavior categories helps in pinpointing which behaviors are appropriate in the light of different objectives. The in step, out of step analysis gives us a general guide which is considerably enhanced by the use of behavior categories. What the analysis of the transcript cannot demonstrate too well is how we can use the language of behavior categories to help us interact more effectively in real dynamic interactions. The remaining chapters in this book attempt to show how the benefits of behavior analysis we described earlier can be achieved on a regular, transaction by transaction basis. Meanwhile, the next chapter gives some more transcripts so that you can have additional practice at categorizing behavior.

SUMMARY

This chapter has examined what is involved in behavior analysis. We have seen that fundamentally behavior analysis is the process of breaking behavior down into smaller elements than usual so that we can be clearer about the influences of various behaviors. We saw that style-level descriptions such as autocratic, democratic, and so on were much too sweeping to give us a clear notion of what was involved in *behaving* the style.

The benefits of behavior analysis were said to be: that they give a precise language for describing what is going on in an interaction; that they are a practicable means of monitoring our own and other people's behavior; that the same language "doubles" as a convenient shorthand when producing a "behavior plan," and, finally, that behavior analysis highlights the shaping effect of certain behaviors on subsequent reactions.

The chapter then went on to concern itself with the first of the four benefits, leaving the others to be explored in later chapters. Some introductory behavior categories were described and applied to the behavior of some participants in a short transcript. The analysis demonstrated how behavior categories help to "tune up" the in step, out of step analysis so that it is possible to pinpoint precisely which behaviors are most appropriate in the achievement of a particular objective.

6

Case Studies on Behavior Analysis

This chapter is included to give you, should you wish it, further practice at using the language of the behavior categories. Having worked through the transcript in the last chapter, and if you feel happy about your ability to use the categories quickly and accurately, you could afford to skip this chapter and move on to Chapters 7 and 8 where we shall see how the categories can be useful in planning and shaping behavior.

Being able to monitor behavior unobtrusively in real interactions is dependent on the skill of analyzing behavior using a language or "labels" of some kind. Whether eventually you choose to use the categories introduced in the last chapter, or to produce some of your own, is immaterial. But the importance of having categories *of some kind* and using them to observe behavior carefully cannot be overstressed. Unless we can monitor behavior accurately, we cannot reach valid conclusions about it; we cannot work out appropriate behaviors and steer clear of inappropriate ones. Everything emanates from the skill of analyzing behavior.

Clearly the transcripts that follow are inadequate in

giving you all the practice you require. In one sense they are easier to analyze because they are less dynamic than a real interaction. You can re-read a contribution, or the whole transcript, if it comes to that, as many times as you like in making your analysis. Obviously, real conversations between people do not lend themselves to this sort of double checking. The analysis has to be on an immediate blow-by-blow, behavior-by-behavior basis. For this reason, I recommend that if you are going to work through the transcripts that follow, you do so by working straight through them fairly swiftly, deciding on the behavior category immediately after each contribution, rather than reading the whole thing through first. It is better to leave the fretting and re-reading for when you check your perceptions with mine.

Perhaps the most serious limitation of written transcripts, making the analysis *more* difficult than with live interactions, is that they only provide information about the actual words that were said. In real life, extra aids to speedy analysis are intonation and accompanying nonverbal behaviors such as facial expressions. Try, therefore, to supplement your analysis of the transcripts with some practice at categorizing behaviors during, say, a play on television. Then move on to categorize real conversations as you yourself take part in them. Half the art of categorizing behavior is to be able to categorize your own contributions as well as those of other people. Transcripts and TV plays will not give you practice at monitoring your own behavior (unless you are actually in them!), so do not spend too long on them before attempting live interactions.

Three transcripts follow. The first is the sequel to the transcript in Chapter 5, but this time is a conversation among only three of the original characters, Frank, Peter, and Mike. The second is a transcript of three conversations between a personnel manager called Chris and one of his personnel officers called Kathy. Finally, there is a transcript of a meeting at a research and development unit of a large organization. All three transcripts are virtually verbatim accounts of real conversations between real people. I have edited them very little, usually only to make exceptionally long contributions more staccato. I have also changed names of both people and organizations. In each case, my categorizations are given at the end of this chapter on pages 138 to 143. It would be best if you recorded your categorizations on scrap paper, together with a note of the number of the contribution.

First Transcript

1. FRANK   Now that we've tried out that new procedure for a few meetings, let's review how well it's working.

2. MIKE   I'm against reviewing it at this stage. It's much too early to review it yet.

3. FRANK   Well—I wanted a review because I'm pretty unhappy about the way things are going and I was anxious to check on your feelings about it before we go any further.

4. PETER   Okay, how about us doing an *interim* review? There's nothing to be lost, surely?

5. MIKE   Yes, I suppose that comparing our impressions now, at this stage, with some more meetings to run, could help us to monitor the remaining trials more thoroughly. I suggest we conduct the review with that sort of benefit in mind.

6. PETER   That's it! Let's agree to conduct this interim review in order to improve the procedure where it already seems to us to be inadequate.

7. FRANK   Okay! Well, since the new procedure was your idea in the first place, Peter, I propose you kick this off and tell us how you think it's going.

8. PETER   I don't agree that it was *my* idea. The final procedure we adopted was more Mike's than mine.

9. FRANK   I merely meant that you were the *originator* of the idea.

10. PETER   I just didn't want Mike's contribution to be overlooked—that's all.

11. FRANK   Fair enough—so how about you starting us off then, Mike?

12. MIKE   I'd like to propose we go ahead with the procedure pretty well unaltered. I feel it's a vast improvement on anything we've tried previously.

13. PETER   My own feelings exactly.

14. MIKE   I am proposing this because it has certainly been successful in helping us to cut down the number of items on the agenda.

15. PETER   I couldn't agree more! It has also been successful in making sure that the things we *do* spend time on during the meeting genuinely concern all of us. I agree with Mike; the procedure doesn't need modification at this stage.

16. MIKE   That's right! People are certainly more involved.

17. FRANK   We aren't going to be able to *improve* the procedure if we just concentrate on its plus points.

18. MIKE   What snags have you got in mind, then?

19. FRANK   Well, I find that, as chairman of the meetings, there are lots of items which don't get discussed that I *want* to have aired.

20. PETER   Do you mean that the meetings aren't as useful from your point of view as they were before?

21. FRANK   That's right. You see, I used the regular meetings as a convenient way of passing messages and checking up on this and that. In fact, I used to come to the meeting with quite a long checklist of small items, and always found that I could dispose of most of them during the meeting.

22. PETER   Well, while we're talking about snags, the only other one I can think of is time. Putting time limits on each agenda item doesn't seem to work. We have always overrun so far.

23. MIKE Well, any suggestions on how to improve the procedure to overcome these difficulties?

24. FRANK From my point of view, I would propose that we scrap it and go back to the way we did things before.

25. PETER That's hardly a suggestion for *improvement*, Frank.

26. MIKE How about us doing a more thorough "pros and cons" exercise on this decision?

27. PETER Yes, I'd prefer to think this through a bit more carefully before agreeing to scrap it.

28. FRANK Okay. How shall we *do* this?

29. PETER I'll collect up the ideas on my pad here. Let's have two columns—one for advantages and one for disadvantages.

30. MIKE Probably better if you do it on the wall board over there, Peter—then we can all see it as the items go up.

31. FRANK Yes—that'll help us to brainstorm. Suppose we just let our ideas flow, and organize them afterwards?

32. PETER I like it.

33. FRANK I'll tell you what. When we've run out of ideas, we can add them up and see if the disadvantages outweigh the advantages—as I suspect they will. If there are more disadvantages than advantages, I propose we automatically agree to scrap the new procedure.

34. MIKE Sounds as if you're pre-judging the outcome, Frank.

35. FRANK No, I'm not! If there *are* more advantages than disadvantages, then I'll go along with it quite happily.

36. MIKE Just a minute—remember that it isn't a question of deciding whether to scrap the procedure or not at this stage. Our purpose in producing this list of ideas is so that we can move on to thinking of ways to overcome the disadvantages we identify.

37. PETER   How about us starting?

38. MIKE   Right—let's record the points we have already mentioned—like an advantage is that the procedure acts as a filter to cut down the number of items on the agenda.

39. FRANK   A disadvantage is that the procedure filters out items that *I* want dealt with at the meeting.

40. MIKE   Another advantage is that the meetings are over quicker.

41. PETER   You know, I'm finding that I can't get all this down *and* come up with my own ideas.

42. FRANK   Well, how about us taking turns at doing the recording, then?

43. PETER   Okay.

44. MIKE   I'm not sure that there *is* much more to record. Suppose we work on this disadvantage of Frank's and leave it at that for now?

45. FRANK   I'd certainly be happy if we could crack that one.

46. PETER   What do you mean when you say *work* on this disadvantage?

47. MIKE   Simply that we try to produce a modification to the procedure which will overcome the snag Frank is worried about.

48. PETER   Any ideas, then?

49. FRANK   Suppose we agreed to have a bit of time set aside for my points as chairman?

50. MIKE   Yes, we could end each meeting with a sort of "chairman's notices" time. Then everyone would be clear that the agenda-setting criteria had been put to one side to give you a special opportunity to raise things which you couldn't otherwise have brought up. Chairman's privilege and all that.

51. PETER   And how about allocating a time limit for that, as we do with the other items of business?

52. FRANK That's great. I think this will overcome my difficulty.

53. MIKE Any ideas on how to introduce this idea to Bill and Tony?

54. PETER Well, Bill is sceptical about the benefits of having a procedure at all, so I'm sure he will see this as the first signs that it's crumbling! I'd just announce it at the start of the next meeting, Frank.

55. MIKE An alternative would be to tell them the problem and see if they can come up with this proposal themselves.

56. FRANK Hmm. I'd feel that was rather rigged, since the three of us have already agreed on it.

57. PETER Okay, then, I take it that you think it's worth getting Bill and Tony to feel committed; so how about starting off the next meeting by describing the difficulty the procedure gives you, Frank? That's the posing the problem bit. *Then* say that we've thought about it and the only idea we've been able to come up with is this one of having a chairman's notices time as an extra to the normal procedure.

58. FRANK Then bring *them* in by asking if they can think of any other way round the difficulty and deliberately involve them in kicking it around a bit.

59. MIKE And if they come up with something better, we can implement that instead.

60. FRANK Done.

Second Transcript

Three short linked conversations between Chris, a personnel manager, and Kathy, one of his personnel officers.

1. CHRIS I've been feeling that we haven't been communicating as well lately, so let's have a chat about it.

2. KATHY   What do you mean, not communicating well?

3. CHRIS   Well, you know, you haven't been to see me so much lately.

4. KATHY   When I *do* come, you don't seem very interested in what I have to tell you.

5. CHRIS   What do you mean by that?

6. KATHY   Well, take last Monday. I was explaining about the recruiting campaign, and as soon as Dickie came in with a question, you switched off and concentrated on that. I just felt that you weren't really interested in what I had to say; in fact, I feel it goes deeper than that. I've noticed that you seem out of touch with what we are doing in the personnel office. It makes me wonder if you really know what is going on.

7. CHRIS   What makes you think that?

8. KATHY   Well, sometimes you ask me to do something in a hurry and seem to have forgotten that I am already tied up. Just last week you asked me to conduct that impromptu survey amongst the secretarial staff when you already knew that I was doing the induction course that day.

9. CHRIS   Okay. A lot of complaints. Shall we take them one at a time and try to agree on some actions to prevent them happening again?

10. KATHY   Good idea.

11. CHRIS   You said that you felt I'm not interested in what you are doing. Any ideas about how that could be overcome?

12. KATHY   Well, a simple action would be for you to resist interruptions when we are having one of our briefing sessions.

13. CHRIS   Hmm. That's easier said than done. I think it would be unwise to ignore a call from the president, for example.

14. KATHY   I think you have just as much of a responsibility toward your own subordinates as you do to the director. It would do him good to have to wait occasionally, anyway. The more you drop everything for him, the worse he gets. Look, this is silly. You asked me for a suggestion, I gave you one, and now you are pouring cold water on it. Can you suggest a *better* idea?

15. CHRIS Sorry, I'm not being very positive, am I? Would you accept a slight modification to your idea? Suppose we said that whenever you are in a meeting with me I stop all interruptions except ones from the president himself? He doesn't come through all that frequently, after all.

16. KATHY Okay, and what about adding that our briefing sessions should take place in my office rather than yours? That would make it easier for you to stick to the "no interruptions" rule as well as giving me and my staff the impression that you were taking an active interest in us.

17. CHRIS Yes, we could even plan briefing sessions between us on a regular basis. Every Monday at 10, or something like that.

18. KATHY I would certainly appreciate that. It would mean that I could save up some items instead of coming through to you all the time with bits and pieces.

19. CHRIS Let me summarize what we have agreed on, then. Every Monday at 10, I am to come to your office for a meeting. I am not allowed to be interrupted except by the director himself.

20. KATHY Would it also be an idea to give ourselves a time limit for those meetings that we would try to stick to except in unusual circumstances?

21. CHRIS Good idea. It means I can schedule the next thing in, knowing that I can make it. What would you think of as an appropriate time limit?

22. KATHY I suppose an hour.

23. CHRIS Fine. That doesn't mean that we have got to

pad out our meetings so that they last an hour, irrespective of what we have to say, does it?

24. KATHY   No, of course not. It just means that neither of us will make any appointments between 10 and 11 on Monday mornings. If our business is over before 11, then that's a bonus.

25. CHRIS   Shall we agree to try that for the next month, and then see if communications between us have improved?

26. KATHY   Yes. I'm sure they will have. This idea of a regular briefing session will help a lot.

[Next Monday morning]

27. CHRIS   Sorry I'm a bit late, I got caught on the stairs coming down.

28. KATHY   Not a very promising start to our new system.

29. CHRIS   I've said I'm sorry. Let's get started now that I'm here. I'll have to leave promptly just before 11.

30. KATHY   But I thought we agreed to hold ourselves free right up till 11?

31. CHRIS   Oh, come on, you're just trying to pick a fight. I suggest we get started and that you kick off with the first thing you have got on your list for me.

32. KATHY   No. I'm sorry, but I think we should get this straight first. I'm still left feeling that you are here under pressure, and that you aren't really interested in what we are doing down here.

33. CHRIS   Look, I've said I'm sorry. I don't want to get caught up in a spiral of recriminations. Let's agree to have four of these meetings, and then review whether they are adequate after that. Keep a list of the things that bug you if you like, but don't bring them up until the review.

34. KATHY   But storing things up on a list isn't as healthy as saying how you feel as you feel it. But in the circumstances I agree to do it that way for the time being.

35. CHRIS Okay! I suggest you make a note of that on your list of things that bug you, and then go ahead and give me the first item you have on today's list.

36. KATHY Well, the first thing is the staffing of the main office. As you know Triss is leaving and Pam obviously will have to go in a couple of months or so. Her baby is due in December.

37. CHRIS Well, one thing is for sure. You can't replace Triss until after the end of the year. We are over our established headcount already.

38. KATHY Do you mean the calendar year's end or the company one?

39. CHRIS The company one, of course. The calendar year has nothing to do with our headcount figures. I'm saying that you can't replace Triss until the beginning of October.

40. KATHY Have you any suggestions about how we can cope until then?

41. CHRIS How about getting in temporary help? Temporaries don't appear on the headcount returns, so you could get in as many of those as you liked.

42. KATHY Well, I don't think that temporaries are any good for our sort of work. I suggest that you do allow us to go ahead and recruit despite the headcount embarrassment.

43. CHRIS I'm sorry, but there is no way that I can agree to that. It's more than my life is worth to be over the top on headcount on the last day of September.

44. KATHY Well, I feel you are being unfair. The only reason you are above establishment is because you took a gamble and brought Joan in, expecting that Susan would have left well before the year end. The difficulty, as I see it, is that you are making us suffer because of that.

45. CHRIS Okay, then. Would it help if I lent you either Joan or Susan until October when we can start recruiting again?

46. KATHY It certainly would, and since for some time now you have suspected that the main office wasn't as busy as we have been claiming, Susan could be conducting a survey of the work load while she is there.

47. CHRIS Okay. I agree to the idea. I'll ask Sue if she would like a spell in the main office.

48. KATHY How will you put the proposition to her?

49. CHRIS Suppose I just ask her if she would mind? Would that do?

50. KATHY Might it be a better idea for *me* to ask her? That way, if she says no, I shall only have myself to blame.

51. CHRIS Good idea. You sound her out and let me know. Then I'll confirm the arrangement with her.

[A month later]

52. CHRIS Well, we promised ourselves a review. I must say I'm well pleased. Have any improvements to the system occurred to you?

53. KATHY I don't know whether I've got any *improvements* to suggest. I still find that you seem to be out of touch with our work load when you ask us to take on extra things.

54. CHRIS How do you mean, out of touch?

55. KATHY Well, the other day, for example, you asked me to get those turnover figures to you pronto and seemed to have forgotten that I was due to interview on the selection panel all that day. Somehow, you have the knack of forgetting what other people have told you they are going to be doing.

56. CHRIS It's a question of priorities. The president was screaming for those figures, and frankly I was surprised that you didn't drop everything to get them to me.

57. KATHY Well, let me give you another example. Joan was saying that she was surprised you hadn't asked her how her father was. You agreed to give her a long weekend so that she could go to see him in the hospital. Then on the Tuesday you called her and remarked that you hadn't been able to find her on Monday! She says that when she reminded you where she had been you just said, "Oh yes" and left it at that.

58. CHRIS You all do gang up on me, don't you?

59. KATHY But I feel we should be able to discuss this sort of thing openly. How about taking this issue and thinking of some proposals to overcome it then?

60. CHRIS Yes, all right. Though I can't for the life of me think of an idea that'll get me to remember what's happening to everyone all the time.

61. KATHY Perhaps we don't have to. What do you say to the idea of producing a plan for getting you to remember *certain* things about *one* person? The plan could just act as an interim discipline to get you into the swing of remembering.

62. CHRIS And once I had started to remember as a habit, the plan would become redundant, you mean?

63. KATHY That's it exactly. Any ideas on what the plan could be?

64. CHRIS Would tying knots in my handkerchief solve the problem?

65. KATHY It would get a bit bulky in your pocket by the end of the day! What about having an arrangement where I tell you what I'm going to be doing each day and test how well you have remembered at the start of the next day?

66. CHRIS Yes, that could do the trick. As I got better at remembering, we could begin to try me over longer periods of time. You know, not daily but weekly, eventually. The test could take the form of me asking how such and such an activity had gone?

67. KATHY That sounds great. We'll have you knowing what your personnel officers actually do in no time!

Case Studies on Behavior Analysis

68. CHRIS   I think we should retain our briefing meetings routine, don't you?

69. KATHY   Yes, and I was wondering if the two assistant personnel officers could come along too?

70. CHRIS   Why not? A good idea. It would make them feel increasingly involved.

Third Transcript

This is a verbatim account of what was said during a regular monthly meeting in a research and development division. This particular R & D unit is organized as a corporate HQ function offering its expertise to a range of product divisions. A couple of years previously, a rumpus was caused when an internal charging system was introduced and the R & D division was asked to recover at least 50 per cent of its costs in receipts, or revenue, each year. This meant that the R & D division was forced to work harder to "win" orders from the divisions in the group in competition with external R & D facilities outside the group. The product divisions are free to decide how much to spend on R & D, whether to form their own specialized R & D units, or, if not, whether to contract the work inside or outside the group.

In the transcript, Dr. Roy is a project manager in the R & D division and the meeting is with four of his direct reporters. They are Harold, Neil, Alan, and Steve. They meet on a regular monthly basis to check on the progress of their various projects.

1. DR. ROY   Does anyone know where Harold is?

2. NEIL   He's around. I saw him at lunch time and he has remembered the meeting because he said something about seeing me at two.

3. DR. ROY   Oh, well! We'd better start without him. I expect he'll be along in a moment. Let's go through the project list, then, checking on progress. Department "X" is first—that's yours, Alan.

4. ALAN   Well, as you know, they are very interested

in finding materials to replace asbestos. They've had people down to look, and I think they are very interested. At the moment they are running some tests themselves to validate the process. If they are successful, the idea is that we would do the remaining bits of development and hand it over to them.

5. DR. ROY I'm a bit suspicious of these people. Back in December they said they'd make up their minds by the end of January. Now it's May!

6. ALAN I think they are about ready for a discussion to plan what to do next. In fact, I'm waiting for them to ring back to say when they want to come.

7. DR. ROY We're going to get pushed out if we aren't careful. I can't see why they need us, can you?

8. ALAN Well, from our point of view there is certainly less in it if they decide to use their own R & D facilities. But I feel they won't want to offend us.

9. DR. ROY Shouldn't we be showing why they need to spend about $10,000 to $20,000 with us?

10. ALAN Well, I think they *must* be interested to have come and looked in the first place.

11. DR. ROY I see. So they are supposed to be coming to talk it over—

12. ALAN That's right. Until then we are as uncertain as everyone else.

13. DR. ROY We'll just have to wait and see. This next one is yours too, Alan.

14. ALAN Yes, well, some samples have been sent. I contacted them a month or so ago and they said they were still thinking about it.

15. DR. ROY You told us that last time. What, if anything, has happened since? Wasn't Bert supposed to have asked them when he went to the other meeting a couple of weeks back?

16. ALAN Yes; I'm not sure whether he did, though.

17. DR. ROY I think so. I'm sure I saw a copy of a

letter. I forget the context just now.

18. ALAN Oh. Well, he must have, then.

19. DR. ROY You'd better check up on that one. They are probably playing for time. Or are we? Don't answer that! Okay! What about the Permatract proposal, Neil?

20. NEIL Well, as you know, they accepted the feasibility study and that was followed up with a proposal worth about $20,000. They say the cash can't be raised this year and that they hope to fit it into next year's budget.

21. DR. ROY Oh, dear! Did you actually go and talk to them about it?

22. NEIL Well, no, it was done on the phone.

23. DR. ROY So you've been spared that one now. And we have been spared $20,000 as well, it seems. Shall we lose it for a bit, then?

24. NEIL Yes, and resurrect it when things are better.

25. DR. ROY All right. This is all very depressing. What about your project, Steve?

26. STEVE Technically there is no doubt we'll get there, as you know. The tests are going very well indeed. The problem is going to be the exploitation. We'll have a product and a mythical market.

27. DR. ROY Yes, but that's their problem, isn't it? We aren't open to any criticism.

28. STEVE Yes, I suppose so. I think I may be being unduly pessimistic. An encouraging sign is that next time they are bringing a marketing consultant with them!

29. DR. ROY I don't know whether that's a good sign or a bad sign. By the way, Steve, what happened about the mysterious coating techniques report? Did it ever turn up?

30. STEVE I'm sure that's really irrelevant in this meeting—but no, I'm still chasing it.

31. DR. ROY I think I'd better have a word with Geoff and see what's happening. I forget when it was I last spoke to them. At least six weeks ago, I think.

32. STEVE So, am I supposed to be chasing that, or you? We'd better be careful we aren't adding to the confusion on that one!

33. DR. ROY You'd better leave it to me. As soon as I get it I'll let you have a copy, naturally.

34. STEVE All right, then. I'd have thought it better if I did it, but still, if you'd rather, it's one less thing for me to do!

[Enter Harold]

35. HAROLD Sorry I'm late. Got stuck talking about the ventilators in the second lab.

36. DR. ROY What did they have to say about them, as a matter of interest?

37. HAROLD Oh! They're all faulty, as I've always said. The whole lot have got to come out and start all over again.

38. DR. ROY Oh, Lord! Wish I hadn't asked you now! How long will it take?

39. HAROLD Well, they *say* a couple of weeks. But I don't believe it! It *ought* to take half that time. But I bet it takes double: four weeks or more, I'd say!

40. DR. ROY Well, I'm sure we can count on you to keep an eye on them and generally push them along. Now, where were we? Oh yes, department Y. Back to you, Neil.

41. NEIL Last time I spoke to them they said to chase them again in the autumn.

42. DR. ROY Okay. Well here's our new little shining light—gas burners. That wasn't supposed to be a joke, but thank you for laughing all the same! Now this one is *really* hopeful. The empirical tests on the new pipes look good. We took one of the prototypes and played a gas flame on it. Then blew cold air down it, and you'd hardly know it had been touched. It was very impressive. Anyway, they now want a quote for us to make up a longer piece of pipe. About 36 inches. If we can pull this off, it could be really big. There are about 200 pipes in each boiler, you see. All we've got to do is make the little things and we're there, I reckon.

43. STEVE What about creep? How do they show up under testing?

44. DR. ROY Well, *they* are doing creep tests. But it's all pretty useless because they won't creep. Still, it gives them something to do.

45. HAROLD I'd like to talk about this manhole cover thing.

46. DR. ROY Right. Fire away!

47. HAROLD I've had a couple of preliminary conversations with them. At present, they use the normal 18 × 24-inch cast iron cover. Or rather, it's a cast iron basket really, filled with 3 or 4 inches of low grade concrete. The problem seems to be that they have to send out more men than are needed for inspection work simply because they are needed to lift the manhole covers! They are asking if we can make manhole covers that are as durable, but light enough for one man to lift.

48. STEVE Do you mean they literally wish us to *make* them? Or to do all the R & D involved in coming up with a new design?

49. HAROLD Well, we couldn't make them could we! We aren't in the production business.

50. STEVE But do we *want* to do this? Do we want to embark on a development program to construct and test an alternative cover?

51. DR. ROY Why not? If there's money in it. How much do the current covers cost to make, Harold?

52. HAROLD The economics aren't straightforward. It isn't just a question of production costs. As I've explained, the present covers cost them *indirectly* in increased labor overheads. One man can't lift the present cover on his own, you see. Or so the unions claim, anyway! But they would, wouldn't they! It's back to "jobs for the boys again," basically!

53. NEIL Have you done any testing on the current covers, Harold?

54. HAROLD Well, we've broken a few using a 6" steel pad to simulate the tire of a truck. The funny thing is that the concrete doesn't seem to make any difference to the strength.

55. NEIL Where *do* they break, in fact?

56. DR. ROY And under what conditions? Centrally loaded with the covers fully or partially supported?

57. HAROLD Look! They aren't going to be impressed with academic stuff! I can tell them enough about how the current ones break—rest assured!

58. NEIL If the concrete doesn't make any contribution, why don't they leave it out and turn them upside down? That would make them lighter.

59. HAROLD Ah! I've misled you there. The iron basket doesn't have a bottom to it. The sides are slightly wedge shaped, you see, and that stops the concrete falling through.

60. DR. ROY It's a St. George's cross, is it, Harold?

61. HAROLD Yes, in cast iron, as I've explained.

62. DR. ROY A St. Andrew's cross would be stronger. I wonder why they don't use a St. Andrew's cross.

63. HAROLD Because the present construction is *strong* enough! They want something equally strong but lighter.

64. STEVE Well I'd like to be clearer about the criteria we need to use to decide whether to get involved in something like this.

65. DR. ROY Suppose we kept the cast iron basket and found a replacement for the concrete filler?

66. NEIL I think that if they just want us to replace concrete with a lighter fill, it's not a technical job for us.

67. HAROLD Not technical? What do you mean? I'll remind you that de-technical is an emotive term around here, with respect, I must disagree totally with you. At least this work could mean we do something really practical and useful for once!

68. DR. ROY Hmm. Must admit I'm still wondering if there is a credible alternative to concrete.

69. NEIL Some kind of plastic dish, perhaps?

70. ALAN Marine ply?

71. DR. ROY Yes, a sheet molded compound. What sort of density material could we offer as an alternative to the concrete?

72. NEIL I'd say 2 as opposed to about 2.5 for low grade concrete.

73. DR. ROY Is that all? Oh, well!

74. NEIL I think you ought to find out if they would accept the same breaking load as now; what the current covers cost to make; what it will save to have a lighter one, and so on. When we know all this, we can sit down and do some unsophisticated calculations.

75. DR. ROY If we are talking about 2 as opposed to 2.5, it is certainly a question of redesigning the whole thing, not just replacing the filler with something lighter, that's for sure.

76. HAROLD Anyway. None of this is helping me much! I'm meeting them early next week. What should I say? Are we interested or not?

77. DR. ROY I should play it by ear for the time being, Harold. You can get an idea of how they are feeling, their enthusiasm, the funding situation, and so on.

78. HAROLD What cost shall I quote, then?

79. DR. ROY You need to break it down into the usual steps. That's why I suggest you play it by ear. You'll soon know whether to put in a bid for a simple feasibility study or whether to mention a bigger package that includes a feasibility study as a first stage only.

80. HAROLD   Okay. I wish the meeting had been a little more *certain* about this. It all seems so vague.

81. STEVE   I'm inclined to agree. I've been sitting back listening to all this, and I really think we ought to spend some time in one of these meetings planning our revenue strategy as a group. I feel that if we five were clearer about our objectives, the criteria we should use to decide whether to go for something or not, and so on, we'd get along far better. As a newcomer, I feel these meetings are very unproductive.

82. DR. ROY   All meetings are unproductive. The real work is what happens in between meetings. This meeting is just supposed to be a monthly check on progress with our revenue earning projects. Nothing more. It's simply a question of working down this list and updating the "comments" column. And that's exactly what we've just done, isn't it?

83. STEVE   No, not really. This thing about the manhole covers hasn't been like that. I felt that Harold wanted some help from us—wanted some decisions. He wasn't merely reporting on progress.

84. DR. ROY   Then Harold was clearly out of order. He shouldn't have brought it up here.

85. HAROLD   With respect, Mr. Chairman, in that case *you* were out of order in allowing the matter to proceed! What is said and not said at a meeting is entirely a function of the chairman.

86. DR. ROY   Oh, I can't accept that! We are all adults. Surely, I'm not supposed to be cracking a big whip around here? That's not my style. I want to operate informally.

87. STEVE   Well, I think it's all right to operate informally providing it's not at the cost of communication confusion, frustration of group members, and so on.

88. NEIL   It seems fair enough, Roy. How about setting some time aside to kick all this around and come up with an agreed *modus operandi*? It couldn't do any harm and it might clear the air a bit.

89. DR. ROY   Very well, if that's what you want. How about you, Alan? You've been very quiet?

90. ALAN   I'm quite happy with things as they are, but I'll go along with the majority on this.

91. DR. ROY   All right! Well, that's settled. We've made a decision! That should make you happier, Harold!

92. HAROLD   Not really. I don't want to sit around deciding how to reach decisions. I just want to get on and do it!

93. DR. ROY   Well, we'll discuss that next time, shall we? Now, anyone got anything else?. . .No? Well, I know it isn't strictly relevant to this meeting but, particularly in view of our discussion just now, I thought you might like to know what we discussed about the corporate plan at the last divisional meeting. The divisional head circulated a paper—I've got it here somewhere, I think; Oh, well, never mind, I can remember the main points. The idea is to have a strategy that can pull all the bits and pieces we do as a division together. Give them some cohesion. The divisional head thinks we should be better at dropping programs that aren't in the main stream, too. He thinks people follow their own inclinations too much without enough consideration of the revenue implications.

94. STEVE   I'm glad you're telling us this, Roy. It's exactly what I was on about earlier—except that it's on a bigger scale. But the considerations are the same. The need for an agreed upon strategy to underpin all we're doing and so on.

95. DR. ROY   The only other point is that the divisional head wants us to move away from getting receipts by doing "nothing" work. He maintains that it isn't good for staff morale just to do odd jobbing to gain credibility.

96. HAROLD   I've been saying that for years! They ought to lay down firm guidelines.

97. DR. ROY   Let's leave it there, shall we? We can take all this up again in our next meeting.

98. STEVE   When will that be, Roy?

99. DR. ROY   Well, a month from now brings us to. . .

100. NEIL   Can it wait that long? Shouldn't we sneak one in earlier since we've identified so many basic issues that need sorting out?

101. DR. ROY   Oh! I'd have thought a month will give us time to meditate.

102. STEVE   How about next Wednesday? I agree with Neil. I don't think it can wait, really.

103. DR. ROY   Next Wednesday is no good for me. I'll be up talking to department W on that day.

104. HAROLD   What about? You haven't mentioned that before, and it isn't on the list!

105. DR. ROY   Whoops! Sorry, I've obviously put my foot in it again. It's a very preliminary inquiry from them at this stage, so I was going to bring it up if and when things became a little more certain.

106. HAROLD   But things don't have to be a dead certainty before they go on our list, do they? I thought the idea was to list *all* our revenue earning projects. Not just those we choose to!

107. NEIL   Let's not take that up now, but it does underline, yet again, the need for us to have a basic sorting out, Roy.

108. STEVE   Is next Thursday any good?

109. DR. ROY   Yes, if it were in the afternoon. How about everyone else? Next Thursday at 2 o'clock, say? Okay? Going, going, gone! Golly! You know what we've done? Agreed to have a meeting about a meeting. I hope it's worth it!

110. HAROLD   So do we!

Behavior Categories for First Transcript

(1) Proposing
(2) Disagreeing
(3) Other behavior (explaining)
(4) Suggesting
(5) Building (on 1 and 4)
(6) Building (on 5)
(7) Proposing
(8) Disagreeing
(9) Other behavior (explaining)
(10) Other behavior (explaining)
(11) Suggesting
(12) Proposing
(13) Supporting
(14) Other behavior (explaining)
(15) Supporting
(16) Supporting
(17) Difficulty stating
(18) Other behavior (seeking information)
(19) Other behavior (giving information)
(20) Seeking clarification
(21) Other behavior (giving clarification)
(22) Other behavior (giving information)
(23) Seeking suggestions
(24) Proposing
(25) Difficulty stating
(26) Suggesting

(27) Supporting
(28) Seeking suggestions
(29) Proposing
(30) Building (on 29)
(31) Building (on 29 and 30)
(32) Supporting
(33) Proposing (possibly building on 29)
(34) Difficulty stating
(35) Disagreeing
(36) Other behavior (recapping on 6)
(37) Suggesting
(38) Other behavior (repeating information given in 14)
(39) Other behavior (repeating information given in 19)
(40) Other behavior (giving information)
(41) Difficulty stating
(42) Suggesting (possibly building on 29/30 but in real life, unless it was specifically flagged, it is unlikely you could link it back that far)
(43) Supporting
(44) Suggesting
(45) Supporting

(46) Seeking clarification
(47) Other behavior
(giving clarification)
(48) Seeking suggestions
(49) Suggesting
(50) Building (on 49)
(51) Building (on 49 and 50)
(52) Supporting
(53) Seeking suggestions
(54) Proposing
(55) Proposing
(56) Difficulty stating
(57) Building (on 55)
(58) Building (on 57)
(59) Building (on 58)
(60) Supporting

Behavior Categories for Second Transcript

(1) Proposing
(2) Seeking clarification
(3) Other behavior
(giving clarification)
(4) Difficulty stating
(5) Seeking clarification
(6) Other behavior
(giving clarification)
(7) Seeking clarification
(8) Other behavior
(giving clarification)
(9) Suggesting
(10) Supporting
(11) Seeking suggestions
(12) Proposing
(13) Difficulty stating
(14) Seeking suggestions
(15) Building (on 12)
(16) Building (on 15)
(17) Building (on 16)
(18) Supporting
(19) Other behavior
(summarizing)
(20) Building (on 17)
(21) Seek suggestions
(22) Proposing
(23) Seeking clarification
(24) Other behavior
(giving clarification)
(25) Suggesting
(26) Supporting
(27) Other behavior
(28) Difficulty stating
(29) Proposing
(30) Difficulty stating
(31) Proposing
(32) Disagreeing
(33) Proposing
(34) Supporting (under
duress!)
(35) Proposing
(36) Other behavior
(giving information)
(37) Proposing
(38) Seeking clarification
(39) Other behavior
(giving clarification)
(40) Seeking suggestions
(41) Suggesting
(42) Proposing

(43) Disagreeing
(44) Difficulty stating
(45) Suggesting
(46) Building
(47) Supporting
(48) Seeking suggestion
(49) Suggesting
(50) Building
(51) Supporting
(52) Seeking suggestions
(53) Difficulty stating
(54) Seeking clarification
(55) Other behavior
(giving clarification)
(56) Other behavior
(explaining)

(57) Other behavior
(giving information)
(58) Difficulty stating
(59) Suggesting
(60) Difficulty stating
(61) Suggesting
(62) Seeking clarification
(63) Seeking suggestions
(64) Suggesting
(65) Suggesting
(66) Building (on 65)
(67) Supporting
(68) Suggesting
(69) Building (on 68)
(70) Supporting

Behavior Categories for Third Transcript

(1) Other behavior
(seeking
information)
(2) Other behavior
(giving
information)
(3) Proposing
(4) Other behavior
(giving
information)
(5) Difficulty stating
(6) Other behavior
(giving
information)
(7) Difficulty stating
(8) Other behavior
(giving

information)
(9) Suggesting
(10) Other behavior
(because it's so
vague)
(11) Seeking
clarification
(12) Other behavior
(giving clarification)
(13) Other behavior (not
explicit enough to
be a proposal)
(14) Other behavior
(giving
information)
(15) Seeking
clarification

(16) Other behavior
(giving clarification)
(17) Other behavior
(giving
information)
(18) Other behavior
(because it's so
vague)
(19) Other behavior
(seeking
information)
(20) Other behavior
(giving
information)
(21) Other behavior
(seeking
information)
(22) Other behavior
(giving
information)
(23) Suggesting
(24) Supporting
(25) Other behavior
(seeking
information)
(26) Difficulty stating
(27) Suggesting
(28) Other behavior
(giving
information)
(29) Other behavior
(seeking
information)
(30) Other behavior
(giving
information)
(31) Other behavior (not
explicit enough to

be a proposal)
(32) Seeking
clarification
(33) Other behavior
(giving clarification)
(34) Supporting (under
duress!)
(35) Other behavior
(36) Other behavior
(seeking
information)
(37) Other behavior
(giving
information)
(38) Other behavior
(seeking
information)
(39) Other behavior
(giving
information)
(40) Other behavior (not
explicit enough to
be a proposal)
(41) Other behavior
(giving
information)
(42) Other behavior
(giving
information)
(43) Other behavior
(seeking
information)
(44) Other behavior
(giving
information)
(45) Proposing (by the
skin of its teeth.
Very vague!)

(46) Supporting
(47) Other behavior (giving information)
(48) Seeking clarification
(49) Other behavior (giving clarification)
(50) Seeking clarification
(51) Other behavior (seeking information)
(52) Other behavior (giving information)
(53) Other behavior (seeking information)
(54) Other behavior (giving information)
(55) Other behavior (seeking information)
(56) Other behavior (seeking information)
(57) Other behavior (!)
(58) Suggesting
(59) Other behavior (giving clarification)
(60) Other behavior (seeking information)
(61) Other behavior (giving information)
(62) Other behavior (giving information)
(63) Other behavior (explaining)
(64) Other behavior (not explicit enough to be a proposal)
(65) Suggesting
(66) Proposing
(67) Disagreeing
(68) Other behavior
(69) Suggesting
(70) Suggesting
(71) Other behavior (seeking information)
(72) Other behavior (giving information)
(73) Other behavior
(74) Proposing
(75) Other behavior
(76) Seeking suggestions
(77) Proposing
(78) Seeking suggestions
(79) Other behavior (explaining)
(80) Difficulty stating
(81) Proposing (but it is very vague. You could be forgiven for thinking it was difficulty stating and/or other behavior!)
(82) Other behavior (explaining)

(83) Disagreeing
(84) Difficulty stating
(85) Disagreeing
(86) Disagreeing
(87) Other behavior
(88) Suggesting
(89) Other behavior (seeking agreement)
(90) Other behavior
(91) Other behavior
(92) Difficulty stating
(93) Other behavior (giving information)
(94) Supporting
(95) Other behavior (giving information)
(96) Supporting
(97) Suggesting
(98) Other behavior (seeking information)
(99) Proposing
(100) Suggesting
(101) Other behavior (explaining)
(102) Building (on 100)
(103) Difficulty stating
(104) Difficulty stating
(105) Other behavior (explaining)
(106) Difficulty stating
(107) Proposing
(108) Suggesting
(109) Other behavior (or difficulty stating?)
(110) Supporting

Footnote on the Categorizations
for the Third Transcript

If you have worked through the third transcript, it will not have escaped your notice that there are a large number of other behaviors! In fact, it works out at about 70 per cent of the total. In my experience this is a suspiciously high level of other behavior in meetings other than pure briefing or information-exchanging ones. Of course, there will always be a need for important behaviors like giving clarification, seeking and giving information, and so on, but, if a discussion wallows in these sorts of behaviors to the exclusion of the others, it is unlikely to finish up having agreed on anything. The discussion will, in effect, have been starved of the behaviors that are involved in thrashing out a sound course of action to which participants can subscribe. If this is to happen, there must be suggestions and proposals and reactions to them (be they building and supporting or disagreeing and difficulty stating). I have found that when participants in a meeting *feel* that it is going round in circles and not really getting anywhere, that correlates with a disproportionate amount of the other behavior. Dr. Roy is a past master at retreating into other behavior just when one of the other categories would have been more productive. The best examples of this are in the first phase of the meeting, up to 44, where time and time again things are left in the air with no actions agreed on because Dr. Roy "retreats" into other behavior. Good examples are 13, 19, and 29; 23 is nearly another example because while it contains a suggested course of action—"Shall we lose it for a bit, then?"—it is hardly a scintillating one in the context of the conversation.

My conclusion on other behaviors is that they are necessary; that they will frequently account for a high percentage of what goes on in an interaction (one reason for this is the obvious one that other behavior is not one category but many and will inevitably occur more frequently therefore); and, finally, that, depending on the objectives of the occasion, if they rise above, say, 50 per cent of the total of all behaviors, it signals the danger of action deprivation. The next chapter on behavior shaping will help you to understand why this should be so.

SUMMARY

In this chapter we have looked at three transcripts of interactions with the object of practicing the skill of monitoring behavior using the language of the behavior categories. I have argued that this is a fundamental skill, since there would be little point in troubling to arrange our behavior in certain ways if we were unable to monitor the effects of having done so. Giving more conscious thought to our behavior in relation to objectives inevitably involves the skill of monitoring our own as well as other people's behavior unobtrusively and accurately.

7

Behavior
Shaping

The way we behave is not a matter of any concern unless it is true that our behavior significantly affects the behavior of those with whom we interact. All behavioral scientists make the assumption that there *is* a link between one person's behavior and another's.

In the first chapter of this book I tried to establish by examples that, since our behavior is by definition always directly observable, it makes a direct impact on the behavior of others. Since then, at intervals throughout the book, I have promised that we shall return to this crucial process and examine it in more depth.

If you fundamentally object to the notion that in many situations the prime object of behaving at all is to influence others, then behavior shaping is not for you! Before you reject it out of hand, however, can I just reiterate that I have no truck with using behavior to manipulate people into positions of acceptance. In part, I object on ethical grounds, and, even leaving that aside, I object because it is patently inefficient. Sooner or later, people know they have been manipu-

147

lated and the resultant cost in resentment, lack of trust, and subsequent suspicion is too high a price to pay. It more than negates any short term gain.

Behavior shaping is not, therefore, some sort of gimmick or an easy ploy to ensure one-upmanship. It is simply a natural extension of the points we have already explored: the easy visibility of behavior; the need to arrange our behavior so that it is appropriate to the objectives of the occasion; the need to monitor our behavior in relation to the reactions and behavior of others.

The word "shaping" in this context is used to describe the process of arranging your own behavior so that it influences (shapes) the behavior returned to you by another person. This process is going on throughout any interaction, whether you are consciously aware of it or not. The gain in making a "natural" process a *conscious* one is that we can harness the behavior shaping processes more effectively. Someone who has learned how to arrange his or her own behavior so that it shapes that of others to mutual advantage is more likely to achieve his or her objectives than someone who has not.

Behavior shaping is, however, by no means a selfish one-sided affair. The likelihood of helping other, perhaps less skilled, people to achieve their objectives and of achieving mutually advantageous outcomes is also greatly increased.

In the first chapter, I gave some simple examples of behavior shaping at work. Most of them were nonverbal—like yawning, smiling, and head nodding. An obvious *verbal* example of the behavior shaping process is found in the relationship between questions and answers. You ask a question and the usual effect is that it will stimulate an answer as a response. If you ask an open-ended question, it will be more likely to "shape" a longer-winded answer than if you ask a closed one, and so on. An example of an open-ended question is: "How are things going in your new job?" A closed question is: "Got a new job, haven't you?" The shaping effect of a question is, not always but usually, to provoke an answer. What, then, of the behavior categories introduced in Chapter 5? What are their behavior shaping roles?

Over the years, I have researched the "cause and effect" links between the different categories on our list by analyzing the sequential patterns in interactions. This is done by a blow by blow analysis of the behavior categories, using abbreviations so that the categories can be captured in the sequence in which they actually occurred. A typical analysis would therefore look like this:

SS	(Seeking suggestion)
P	(Proposing)
DS	(Difficulty stating)
E	(Explaining)
B	(Building)

After analyzing a few hundred interactions of various kinds, I do a count to discover which behavior follows which most frequently. From these findings, I begin to build up a picture of the behaviors that are instrumental in evoking certain responses. In this chapter, I am going to share the findings with you because they form the basis for those of us who wish consciously to arrange our behavior, not just with an eye on safeguarding our objective, but also with some regard for its effect on the behavior of others.

Actually, I am not sure that it makes sense to distinguish between safeguarding objectives and shaping the behavior of others. For me, the two are inextricably intertwined. In interaction, I cannot really see how it is possible to achieve your objective, other than fortuitously, without paying careful regard to the interplay between your behavior and that of those with whom you are interacting. I hope I have demonstrated this by showing how frequently a large chunk of our success in interaction is determined by the behavioral reactions of others. This is why I have emphasized the importance of including behavioral standards as part of the end of interaction objective. If you care to look back at some of the illustrations of objectives in earlier chapters, you will see how often a substantial element is concerned with whether or not we, through our behavior, brought about certain observable reactions in others. Often, they are spontaneous utterances about the usefulness of the interaction from their point of view. You may object that people do not say what they mean ("never meaning what they say, never saying what they mean" goes the pop song) frequently enough to make these a significant guide to success. But remember that we only have access to their overt behavior and must use it as best we can as an indirect "window" on what they really think or feel beneath the behavioral surface.

"Actions speak louder than words" it is often claimed; but in interactions, words are frequently the closest we can hope to get to actions. In any case, if we can influence people impressively enough during an interaction, we stand a good chance of closing the gap between actions and words. If people leave an interaction deeply committed to doing something, so deeply committed that they *say so* as they leave, they are more likely to do it than if they leave unimpressed and saying they will do something as a means of securing their early exit. If only we could shape behavior more effectively, cynical comments such as "When all is said and done, far more is said than done" need never have any bite again. Let us go through each of the behavior categories, pinpointing their behavior shaping effects. Most of my research findings should accord with your own experiences, because I am only quoting from the sequential monitoring done while observing real, on the job, interactions. I have been careful to keep separate the stockpile of observations from "artificial" interactions that took part on training programs. This is because interactions on contrived behavior change programs are not necessarily representative of what happens in interactions in the normal work place.

THE BEHAVIOR SHAPING EFFECTS
OF THE BEHAVIOR CATEGORIES
INTRODUCED IN CHAPTER 5

Seeking Proposals/Suggestions

The most likely reaction to this behavior is, as you might expect, a suggestion or proposal. Statistically, a proposal is more likely than a suggestion simply because proposals (in the strict sense in which we differentiate between them and suggestions; see Chapter 5, page 102) occur at least twice as often as suggestions. Seeking clarification also figures as a possible reaction, but it is not nearly as likely as a proposal or suggestion.

Seeking proposals/suggestions is therefore a powerful shaping behavior, since it is relatively easy to predict its effects accurately. Even so, these outcomes cannot be *guaranteed*. We are merely observing that it is statistically highly probable that proposing, suggesting, or, a long way behind, seeking clarification will occur in the wake of this behavior. If, for example, the person you are interacting with hasn't got a clue, you can seek suggestions till you are blue in the face and still draw a blank. Behavioral skills do not compensate for empty headedness!

Proposing

Reactions to a proposal divide equally into two camps; either the reaction is supporting, or, equally likely, difficulty stating. Which way it goes seems more dependent on the perceived quality of the proposal itself and less to do with the way in which it has been expressed. Those who see the content of the proposal as sound will react to it supportively, and those who see it as half-baked in some way will react by pointing out the problems and snags.

151

Seeking clarification, disagreeing, and building—in this order—are also quite possible immediately after a proposal, but the figures show supporting and difficulty stating to be far and away the most probable.

Suggesting

The fascinating distinction between suggesting and proposing is that suggestions edge supporting ahead of difficulty stating as a reaction. In other words, if you put an idea forward as a proposal, you run a greater risk of running into difficulties than if you put the very same idea as a suggestion. Furthermore, even if your idea is inadequate, expressing it as a suggestion makes it more likely that people will build on it than expressing it as a proposal.

So suggesting is an important alternative to proposing when you are in a situation where your objective puts a premium on securing agreement. Again, I should warn that behavior shaping is not magic; suggestions still get clobbered with difficulty stating and disagreeing! We are talking about arranging our behavior to make it as likely as possible that it has the desired effect on other people. Even if we fail, we shall do so having done all we could to succeed; and that is the best that anyone can do.

Seeking clarification and disagreeing, in this order, are also quite possible in the wake of a suggestion, just as they were after a proposal.

Building

The most likely response is supporting. This is even more likely than for a straightforward suggestion. Seeking clarification and building, practically neck and neck, come next. But there is an important proviso in claiming that these are the most probable reactions after building: If they are to apply, the build must have been perceived as one by the reactors. It is no good perceiving it as a build yourself and leaving those you are interacting with in the dark. They may well fail to link your build to an earlier suggestion or proposal, in which case the chances are they will react to it as an *alternative* proposal or suggestion. This is particularly hazardous, and, should this happen, the likelihood of disagreeing and difficulty stating is high.

To some extent, this proviso applies to all our behavior. Clearly, if people aren't clear what we are up to behaviorally, the risks that they will interpret it "wrongly" (in our perception), are much greater. The solution is to "flag" your behavior frequently and certainly to be careful to "flag" builds since they are extra risky. By "flagging" I literally mean including a behavioral commentary in your contribution. This does not mean using the "jargon" of the category labels (unless you are lucky enough to be interacting with someone who uses them also, in which case they won't be jargon: jargon is in the eye of the beholder), nor need it be laborious. Here are some examples of "flagging" using everyday parlance:

"This is an idea off the top of my head. . ." (suggesting)

"I'd like to put up a trial balloon" (suggesting)

"I propose that. . ." (proposing)

"I've just been thinking about Bill's earlier idea that we. . .I'd like to add to it by suggesting. . ." (building)

"I like that idea! Can I develop it further by proposing. . ." (building)

"I'd like to say something in support of that" (supporting)

"I'd like to play devil's advocate with that idea for a few minutes" (difficulty stating)

"I'm going to disagree with that and explain why" (disagreeing)

"Could I just check that I have got this straight? As I understand it you are suggesting that. . ." (seeking clarification)

This is not an exhaustive list. You may realize that you have some characteristic phrases that you use to give this sort of behavioral guide to people. What is fatal is to flag a piece of behavior incorrectly. People will often say, "I'd like to develop that idea a bit. . ." and then go on to put up an alternative that isn't a development at all.

My conclusion is that flagging, providing it is correct, is enormously helpful in a conversation because it helps to shape people's perception of behavior and, in consequence, their reactions. I have noticed that the tendency to give an explicit behavioral pointer correlates with other interactive skills and successes. I am satisfied that flagging is one of the outward signs of interactive competence. (See the last chapter in this book.)

So, to return to building specifically, *if* it is recognized as a build, the likelihood of support is very high. The other fascinating thing is that building, as a *reaction* to a build, occurs more frequently than at any other time. It seems that builds beget builds, and there can be quite a chain of them, often in short, excited bursts. Many brainstorming techniques recognize this and try to create behavioral conditions where creativity (behaviorally, that is to say, producing lots of "good" suggestions, proposals, and builds) can flourish. It is particularly interesting that so many brainstorming techniques explicitly forbid reactions of the difficulty stating and disagreeing kind. This is an example of a behavior plan, and we shall turn our attention to such matters in the next chapter.

Disagreeing

Very definite in its behavior shaping effects. The aggressive reaction is to disagree back. The defensive reaction is to retreat into other behavior by trying to explain the disagreement away. I have watched people get sucked into the disagree-disagree spiral many times. It is particularly prevalent in management and trade union negotiations, and, on the domestic front, between husband and wife. This is not to condemn disagreeing. It can be a useful way to sort things out. Indeed, in our culture, there are signs that we put high value on disagreeing as a behavior. Most debating procedures, be they in the university, the Congress, or on television, are deliberately structured to promote disagreement. This serves to remind us that whether disagreeing is appropriate or not depends on circumstances and objectives. Sometimes it is stimulating behavior that paves the way to getting people to change their minds about something. Sometimes it is a pointless, destructive behavior that ends up in an entrenched mud-slinging match.

Supporting

Seems to act as a behavioral fertilizer. It either encourages more suggestions/proposals or, much more likely, it has the effect of so heartening the person being supported that he says his idea all over again! Supporting is therefore most frequently followed by an often lengthy piece of other behavior. This is likely to be the response even if repetition of the idea is superfluous. So verbal support acts in much the same way as nonverbal support such as head nodding and other signals of approval; all push up reiterations whether they have been explicitly called for or not. Supporting is a particularly useful behavior, therefore, if you are in a situation where you want to encourage people to participate. It is not an appropriate behavior if you are trying to curtail someone who is verbose!

Difficulty Stating

A fascinating behavior which is widespread but totally uncertain in its behavior shaping effects. I have observed literally thousands of difficulty stating behaviors and still no clear response pattern emerges. These, however, are the most likely:

a. *Seeking suggestions:* This occurs when someone reacts to the difficulty stating by saying something like "So what would *you* suggest then?"

b. *Proposing/suggesting/building* all often occur immediately after difficulty stating, particularly when difficulty stating is used in the devil's advocate way. This is useful in provoking better ideas that overcome the difficulties, providing the participants are capable of coping in this way. But often people cannot, and one of the reactions listed below is then more typical.

c. *Disagreeing and/or other behavior* happens when people cannot cope with the difficulty by producing a proposal that removes it or by seeking a proposal that, in effect, turns the tables. Instead, they react to difficulty stating precisely as if it were a disagreement, failing to discriminate between the two (a monitoring failure). If aggressive, they disagree with the difficulty that has been pointed out; if defensive, they try to explain it away.

d. *Seeking clarification* is the final significant reaction we need to note following difficulty stating. Seeking clarification is often a prelude to producing some ideas aimed at overcoming the difficulty. The sequence is often like this:
Proposing——difficulty stating——seeking clarification——giving clarification——new/better proposal.

My conclusion from this host of likely responses is that difficulty stating is a particularly dodgy behavior, in the sense that its effects are so unpredictable. Difficulty stating is a good example, therefore, of a behavior that needs to be flagged explicitly, so that it is not perceived as disagreeing, and used judiciously, ensuring that it is in step with objectives.

Seeking Clarification

Very certain in its effects; it usually stimulates giving clarification. It is, therefore, a powerful shaping behavior. But there is a complication. Again, it has basically to do with whether seeking clarification is perceived as such by the person with whom we are interacting. If it is perceived as something other than seeking clarification, obviously the behavior shaping effects alter accordingly. Suppose, for example, seeking clarification was perceived as "disagreeing without actually saying so." Examples are: "So you are suggesting that we do so and so are you?" "Tell me, what would happen if so and so occurred?" and many more. When this happens, it is quite possible for disagreeing to be the reaction rather than giving clarification, as the behavior shaping process predicts.

Once again, we see the need to transmit behaviors that are perceived in the way in which we intend so that behavior shaping can help in controlling the conversation. Seeking clarification is hazardous here because the motives or objectives in using the behavior can vary so much. You can seek clarification in order to become clear, disagree without actually saying so, get the other person to spot the snags and difficulties for himself without having to difficulty state yourself, buy time, and so on. An interactively skilled person uses it to become clear and uses alternative behaviors to meet other objectives. For example, "counseling" someone to discover the snags in their idea for themselves is more honestly and effectively done by a combination of difficulty stating and seeking suggestions.

Other Behavior

The most likely reaction is some more other behavior! For this reason, whole chunks of an interaction can be other behavior and little else. It has a sort of risk-free, cosy attraction about it that the other behaviors are lacking. If you seek a suggestion, for example, then you have really started something and triggered off a chain of behaviors that may lead to commitment to some course of action. There is no such danger with other behavior! The attractions of seeking and giving information, explaining things, clarifying things, repeating things *ad infinitum* are too tempting for many meetings and discussions.

Apart from other behavior stimulating other behavior, the data show no clear cut pattern. In other words, if other behavior is not the response, virtually any of the other categories can be. This makes other behavior a particularly inept behavior to indulge in *if*, and this is a vital proviso, you are in a situation where you need to work hard at persuading or influencing. In these sorts of situations, you need to retain control of the conversation, and the most in step behaviors are therefore the more potent behavior shaping ones. To wallow in other behavior is out of step and leaves you vulnerable, since it is not a powerful shaper and since it leaves your adversary relatively free to select his next response (providing he can survive the temptation to produce some more other behavior).

CONDITIONS UNDER WHICH BEHAVIOR SHAPING WORKS BEST

There are conditions under which behavior shaping thrives. Some of them are rather obvious and are remarkably similar to the conditions under which face to face communications of any kind go well. For example, one of the requirements for behavior shaping is that the people you are interacting with are listening adequately. If they do not listen, then, quite clearly, the behavior shaping effects we have just listed do not happen. Not only this, but, as everyone knows, the *content* of what is being communicated also suffers. On this point, it is worth adding that, while it is popular to think of communication problems as a *content* issue, many so-called communication problems are actually confusions over behavior rather than content. How often have you been overcome with a kind of fuzzy uncertainty about what someone is up to? You understand the content of what he says, but that still leaves you ambiguous about his motives. "Does he already know the answer and is testing me or is he genuinely seeking to know?" "Has he deliberately left that unsaid?" "Is he assuming that I know he knows I know?" I admit to experiencing these feelings of ambiguity quite frequently. Some senior managers are absolute masters of communication by innuendo. Even if you try to pin them down by seeking clarification, they still seem able to slip out of focus and return to sentences that fade out before they are completed, *implied* suggestions and proposals, and a smoke screen of "other behaviors."

Another condition that seems necessary for behavior shaping to operate successfully is that the people you are interacting with are sane! This may sound facetious, but sanity is quite definitely a prerequisite. Perhaps one of the hallmarks of an insane person is that behavior shaping effects cannot be observed in his reactions and that, irrespective of what behavior is presented, he insists upon jumping off at tangents. Clearly this is an appalling oversimplification, since the word "insane" is genetic and covers a whole variety of disorders. There are some people who, despite clearly transmitted behaviors, ignore them and produce unrelated reactions. Perhaps you know a few like that? Certainly they are enormously difficult to do business with!

A third condition under which behavior shaping works best relates to the number of people involved in the interaction. Even if we are fortunate enough to be interacting with sane listeners, behavior shaping becomes increasingly difficult in direct relation to the number of people participating in an interaction. The most favorable conditions for behavior shaping are undoubtedly interactions between two people only. As soon as there are additional participants, complications begin to set in which confuse the sequence of behaviors. I have often speculated that one of the criteria to apply in deciding whether a group is interacting as a *team* or not is to map the behaviors sequentially and, if it reads exactly as if only two people were in conversation, that would be a legitimate measure of teamwork! The confusion with most groups is that, in effect, there is more than one conversation going on in parallel. Rather like this:

> Person A asks for suggestions.
>
> Person B responds with a suggestion.
>
> Person C ignores B's suggestion and puts a suggestion of his own.
>
> Person A supports B's suggestion.
>
> Person B is encouraged and says his suggestion all over again!
>
> Person C is very puzzled about what happened to his suggestion and seeks clarification.
>
> Person D speaks for the first time to build on C's suggestion.
>
> Person B explains the merits of his suggestion.
>
> Person C, encouraged by D's build, says *his* suggestion all over again! And so on!

If we unravel this, it is clear that persons A and B are in conversation with one another, and so are persons C and D; but they are having two separate and yet interspersed conversations. Add more people and even more separate conversations can break out. If group interactions like this are merely monitored sequentially without also noting the identity of the speaker, behavior shaping effects fail to appear. It is only when the separate conversations are unraveled that the behavior shaping effects emerge.

The final condition to be mentioned follows directly from the previous three. It is that behavior shaping works best when the people interacting are interactively skillful. Precisely what is meant by this is explained in the final chapter; it suffices to say at this point that the more those interacting subscribe to the view that their behavior is important in shaping the outcome of the interaction, and are consciously monitoring behavior and striving to arrange it appropriately, the better behavior shaping works. This is the corollary to the earlier points about adequate levels of listening, sanity, and behavior flagging. It reminds us that interactive skills are not an exercise in one-upmanship. The more participants are behaviorally enlightened, the more *mutual* success will be sought and achieved. This is why genuine teamwork is a rare occurrence. It requires each individual member of the team to share behavioral responsibility for its success. Most people prefer to shrug this responsibility onto the team leader by putting him "in charge" of keeping behavioral order. If things go wrong, it is his fault. In a *team*, the leader is out of a job most of the time because the individual participants are capable of ordering their own behavior appropriately.

BEHAVIOR "POWER"

Our analysis has already shown that some behaviors are more "powerful" than others in the sense that they are more influential in shaping a predictable reaction. Seeking suggestions/proposals and seeking clarification are "powerful" behaviors, therefore, since reactions to them are as certain as anything can be in this imprecise behavioral area!

If we tidy up the behavior shaping findings, an interesting pattern begins to emerge. Let us give ourselves two axes. The first a shaping—responding one with the behaviors that are *more* concerned with shaping the next behavior plotted at one end and the behaviors *more* concerned with reacting to the previous behavior at the other. This gives us:

SHAPING BEHAVIORS	RESPONDING BEHAVIORS
Seeking suggestions/ proposals	Disagreeing
Suggesting	Supporting
Proposing	Difficulty stating
Building	Other behaviors
Seeking clarification	

There are two problems with this split. One is that difficulty stating in particular, *if* it is flagged explicitly, *can* in certain circumstances, be a powerful shaping behavior (when playing devil's advocate, etc.). The other is that building and seeking clarification are hybrids, really, in that they are both, at one and the same time, reactions to a previous behavior *and* shapers of the next. You can either consider this a crippling embarrassment to the classification system, or, more fruitfully, you can note that this tells us something "special" about building and seeking clarification. To produce a shaping-responding behavior in one fell swoop is a useful thing to be able to do, as will be shown in the next section of this chapter.

If we now reshuffle the behaviors with a second axis in mind, this time splitting the seeking and nonseeking behaviors (seeking are those where a question is asked, nonseeking is when a statement is made) we get:

SEEKING BEHAVIORS	NON-SEEKING BEHAVIORS
Seeking suggestions/ proposals	Proposing
	Building
Suggesting	Disagreeing
Building	Supporting
Seeking clarification	Difficulty stating
Other behavior (seeking information, seeking confirmation/agreement)	Other behaviors (giving clarification, explanation, information, etc.)

Notice that building appears in both lists because it can either be done the suggesting way or the proposing way and still be essentially a build, of course. Strictly speaking, we need to split building into two categories: "suggesting-building" and "proposing-building"; but if we start doing that, before we know it we shall have more categories than we can usefully cope with.

Finally, if we pull the two axes together into one "model," we can pinpoint the power of different behaviors.

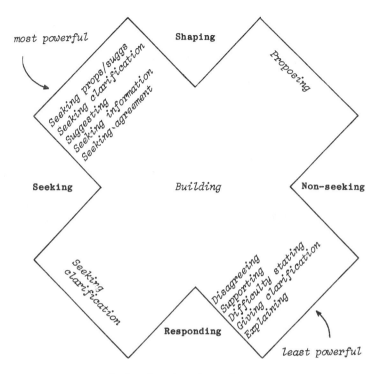

most powerful

Shaping

Seeking props/suggs
Seeking clarification
Suggesting information
Seeking agreement

Proposing

Seeking

Building

Non-seeking

Seeking
clarification

Disagreeing
Supporting stating
Difficulty clarification
Giving clarification
Explaining

Responding

least powerful

From a behavioral point of view, we can conclude that in any interaction the person who uses most seeking-shaping behaviors is being the most powerful. Conversely, the person who uses the most nonseeking-responding behaviors is being the least powerful. Behaviors housed in the remaining arms of the St. Andrew's cross come somewhere in between.

IMPLICATIONS OF
BEHAVIOR SHAPING

By now, you should be asking: "So what?" "What difference is this going to make?" and similar questions showing scepticism.

My answer, inevitably, takes us to the heart of the matter, since behavior shaping is at the center of all that is involved in interactive skills. Behavior shaping is quite literally what it's all about: the business of consciously arranging your own outward display of behavior so that it has the desired effect on the behavior of those with whom you are in face to face encounter. As I have said before, the whole of behavioral science pivots on the assumption that behavior can and does occupy this central role.

Behavior shaping therefore encapsulates all that is involved in deciding which behaviors to employ, how frequently, and in what "mix" in a given interaction. As we discovered earlier, the starting point for this decision is the situation itself, closely followed by our determination to achieve an end-of-interaction objective. In some situations, armed with certain objectives, we would wish to control our behavior so that we hung on to the shapers: whenever we are "up against it" and wish to increase the probability of persuading others to our point of view, for example; or whenever we are in a situation where the objectives of individual participants are in conflict, or where we want to "clinch" agreement to a specific course of action, to mention two more. In other situations, it is perfectly acceptable to indulge in a predominance of nonseeking-responding behaviors. A classic example of when it is appropriate to do this is when you are in interaction with someone whose objectives, while different in detail from yours, are so similar that you can afford to fall in line behind his behavior and still achieve the objective to which you are committed. There is no point in having a power struggle for the shapers unless your objectives are in real jeopardy.

In no sense, therefore, am I arguing that the seeking-shaping behaviors are "good" and the nonseeking-responding behaviors are bad. It is the same old argument. There is a time and a place for all the behaviors. The situation and your objectives will tell you when and where.

Having reminded ourselves of that, let us explore some of the implications of behavior shaping in more depth.

The first implication is that we must learn to generate behaviors that are perceived in the way in which we intend if the behavior shaping predictions are to come true. This is the old transmission and reception problem inherent in any sort of communication. Since human beings are so complicated, they will insist on processing incoming information by giving it meanings which are not always there. This is known as the perceptual process, and it can play havoc with what would otherwise be "straightforward" observations of the world about us. The only safeguard to which you, as a transmitter of a piece of behavior, can have recourse is that of explicitly labeling or flagging your behavior to maximize the probability that it will be received as you intended. We looked earlier at some of the everyday turns of phrase used when flagging behavior. Quite clearly, if our build, say, is perceived as difficulty stating, then the behavior shaping effects will be as for difficulty stating and not for building.

A second implication is that the more we "mix" the behavior categories in one piece of behavior, the more we are likely to leave the receiver in a muddle about the bit to which he should respond. For example, if we say: "Now, what ideas have you got to suggest? I was thinking it might be preferable to. . .But of course the snag with that would be. . .Or alternatively we might do so and so. . .at least that would have the advantage of. . ." we have overburdened the receiver. In general, the more we burden him with a choice, the more we risk damaging the behavior shaping effects. This argues for disciplining ourselves to arrange our behavior in more or less single-category-at-a-time contributions. This has the spin-off merit of forcing most people to be less long-winded; but it is obviously not a guarantee, because it is quite possible to prevaricate at length and still only use one category! Other behavior is particularly perilous from this point of view.

The final important implication is that behavior shaping not only indicates which behaviors we should use to make it as likely as possible that we achieve the objective (the next chapter takes the whole issue of planning "in step" behaviors further); it also helps us to be clear about the sort of behavioral antidotes we can use (if we must) to counterbalance the undesirable effects of other people's behavior on us. Behavior shaping is not a one way process, and unless we monitor behavior consciously we can get caught in the slipstream created by someone else's behavior. This is exactly what was happening to David in the transcripts we looked at earlier (Chapter 2, pp. 35–39; Chapter 3, pp. 47–53).

Let me give you some examples of how it is possible to counteract the undesirable effects of other people's behavior. In doing so, they are not offered as golden rules, nor as a recipe for winning, if winning means that the others present do not achieve their own objectives. But when we are interacting with unenlightened people who are jeopardizing the achievement of mutually beneficial objectives, "ploys" such as the following seem justified.

How to avoid being tempted into the disagreeing spiral. When someone disagrees with you, pretend to yourself that they are merely difficulty stating and not actually disagreeing. This has the advantage of making it much more likely that your response is "constructive." If you imagine he is difficulty stating, for example, you can try to produce a suggestion or proposal to overcome the difficulty rather than be tempted into aggressively disagreeing back or defensively trying to explain the disagreement away.

How to cope with pathological difficulty starters. There are people who are so analytical that they predominantly difficulty state whenever they react to someone else's ideas, suggestions, or proposals. It almost seems as if some deep seated principle forbids them to support or build. Such people can be useful in keeping us up to scratch by acting as a sounding board. On many occasions, however, this habit can be enormously depressing and unproductive. There are two antidotes. One puts the onus on you; the other puts the onus on them. The first is to pretend that their difficulty state is an invitation to build. The second is to respond by concurring with their difficulty state and asking *them* for a suggestion/proposal. If this works, it succeeds in getting them in a proposing and you in a responding mode: a complete reversal of the state of affairs that existed previously.

How to avoid disagreeing or difficulty stating yourself. The answer is to build instead. This is not as difficult as it might seem, since, if you think about it, you will realize that whenever you difficulty state you are half way to building anyway. Building is an extra thought process tacked on to a difficulty stating one. Few people seem able to produce a build without thinking or talking their way through a difficulty state first.

How to avoid losing control of the conversation. The best way is to hang onto your fair share of the shaping behaviors. This does not mean blatantly ignoring any of the shaping behaviors other people present to you, but it does mean disciplining yourself to finish your reply with a shaper. For example, if you are giving clarification because it has been sought, you should add, say, a suggestion so that their behavior is shaped accordingly. As we have seen, many of the "other behaviors" are particularly sloppy in their shaping effects. The answer is to conclude with one of the shapers and never to permit yourself to indulge in other behavior *by itself.* Remember that building and seeking clarification are ways of responding with a shaper. This hybrid characteristic makes them particularly useful behaviors when trying to retain control of the conversation.

How to get people to agree with you. The answer shone through the behavior shaping data cited earlier. The most likely way to get agreement is to put your idea forward as a suggestion rather than a proposal. Better still, if you can build on someone else's idea, support is extremely likely. You can "arrange" building opportunities for yourself by seeking suggestions/proposals and then disciplining yourself to build on the ones that come in response.

This is not a comprehensive list of behavioral antidotes. Once you start thinking in terms of behavior categories and behavior shaping, all sorts of other discoveries are possible.

SUMMARY

Chapter 7 has explored the concept of behavior shaping, which was defined as the process of arranging your own outward display of behavior so that it has the desired effect on the behavior of those with whom you are in face to face encounters. We looked briefly at the ethics of consciously doing this, and noted that interactive skills is not synonymous with one-upmanship, manipulation, or the like—quite the reverse in fact.

The bulk of the chapter was spent examining the precise shaping effects of the behavior categories introduced earlier in Chapter 5. This led us to see that some behaviors were more significant shapers than others, that sane listeners are an invaluable aid to the process, and that the onus is on us to transmit really clear behaviors.

Our analysis gave us a four-way model, with shaping and responding behaviors on one axis, and seeking and nonseeking behaviors on the other. This helped us to see that some behaviors clustered together as more "powerful," in a behavior shaping sense, than others. Whether to be primarily shaping or responding during an interaction could only be decided in the light of objectives.

The final section of the chapter looked at some of the "antidotes" that you can use (when you must) to protect yourself against some of the undesirable influences of other people's behavior.

8

How to Plan Behavior

Inevitably, we have already touched on behavior planning on the way to this penultimate chapter. Let us draw the various strands together before looking more carefully at what is involved in planning and controlling behavior.

At intervals through the book, there have been hints about when and when not to plan. In general, the guidance has always looked back to objectives and the circumstances of the situation in which you find yourself. I have argued that whenever you are in a face to face encounter and conscious of wishing to achieve an objective, the way you behave matters. It is under these conditions that troubling to plan, arrange, and control behavior is advisable. The actual objective may vary considerably, but, in general, if you want to influence and/or impress, then conscious monitoring, planning, and controlling should cut in.

There are circumstances where impressing and/or influencing are extra tough, and I find it useful to have three factors particularly in mind. The first is time: the less of it, or, in other words, the shorter your face to face contact, the more difficult it is to impress and/or influence. Every door to door salesman knows that. A second factor relates to objectives. When the people involved in the interaction have *conflicting* objectives, it is more difficult to impress and/or influence. Every negotiator has experience of that. Thirdly, when the situation is emotionally charged, with feelings running high, it is more difficult to impress and/or influence. Every husband or wife in the middle of a fight knows that.

In earlier chapters, there have also been passing references to the link between the language of behavior categories and planning itself. In Chapter 5 the point was made, but not expanded, that one of the benefits of breaking behavior down into small "bits," such as categories, was that it gave us a "shorthand" when thinking about how best to behave in the light of a particular situation and desired objective. Also, in Chapter 5, I was rash enough to claim that the "secret" in actually adapting our behavior and stretching our behavioral repertoire was to plan behavior around behavior categories rather than vague intentions. This chapter makes these points more convincingly, and shows how to plan behavior in the light of objectives.

WHAT IS A PLAN?

A plan—for *any* activity, not just for interactions—is a detailed expression of a predetermined course of action. Some plans are predetermined well in advance of implementation; others are pieced together more hurriedly, immediately before implementation. This links back to a point made in Chapter 2 about preparatory planning and on-going planning. Preparatory planning is fine if you are lucky enough to *have* a beforehand during which to do the predetermining. On-going planning is necessary in the rough and tumble of all those interactions that "just happen" with no, or inadequate, prior warning. Provided it is detailed, predetermined, and a course of action, it is a plan. In the transcript we looked at in Chapter 5, Peter was an example of someone who was putting into action a plan he had put together *before* the meeting; Mike was an example of someone who hurriedly analyzed the situation, did some on-going planning, and, as it happened, went on to win the laurels as the most effective participant in the discussion! *When* we plan—whether hours or split seconds before action—does not matter. That we do so, thus disciplining our behavior in the light of objectives, is all that matters.

Let us look at a couple of plans to see if they are detailed expressions of predetermined courses of action.

A domestic one first: Suppose I notice that when my children suggest involving me in some game or another, my reaction is to decline the invitation more often than I accept it. And suppose I notice that this has a dampening effect on the children and leads to complaints from my wife. Given these conditions, I may conclude that it is desirable to make a behavior change. In order to do this, I need a plan. It need not be complicated, but it must be fairly detailed so that I can put it into action when the need arises. My plan might be:

Whenever the children suggest that I join them in playing a game, I will respond by saying an unhesitating "yes" on 100 per cent of occasions. I will follow the "yes" up with a question about the rules/form of the game and listen to the explanation they give. If the proposed game is hazardous to property and likely to lead to breakages inside or outside the house, or hazardous to limb and likely to end in physical injury or tears, then I'll suggest enough amendments to the rules to reduce these objections. On at least 50 per cent of occasions, I must play the game *there and then*, but always with an agreed time limit! On the remaining occasions, I must at least have planned with the children when we are going to play the game and pinpointed *when* fairly precisely i.e., not "sometime next week" but rather "on Tuesday evening as soon as I get in and have read the paper for a maximum of 15 minutes!")

The onus is now on me to stick to my plan, and if I do I shall succeed in changing my "no" reaction in these circumstances. This will please me, my children, and my wife!

Here is another example of a plan, this time a work-related one. It is a relatively well known problem-solving procedure that aims to make it likely that groups of people will be able to work together and generate feasible solutions to problems. Throughout the following description of the plan, the person who owns the problem and wants the participants to help him solve it is referred to as the "client." Another key person in the plan is called the "leader." He is the custodian of the procedure and ensures that participants stick to it, even if they find it a strain to do so at times. In essence, the plan is as follows:

Step 1.   The client states what he thinks his problem is. It is written up on a flip chart pad where everyone can read it.

Step 2.   The client speaks about the problem, giving the minimum background information he believes is necessary.

Step 3.   The participants ask the client questions of clarification which they feel are vital to qualify them for the next step.

Step 4.   The participants are invited to restate the problem, but restatement must be phrased as "How to (do so and so)?" and are therefore positive, action oriented questions. The leader records all these verbatim on flip charts.

Step 5.   The leader invites the client to pick a restatement of the problem which appeals to him as a worthwhile avenue of exploration.

Step 6.   Participants are invited to give ideas and to try to build on one another's ideas in relation to the selected statement. All ideas are recorded on flip charts by the leader.

Step 7.   At intervals, the leader asks the client to say

what he thinks is good about a listed idea. After this, the leader asks him to state his concerns and doubts, but always in the form: "How to (overcome such and such a difficulty)?"

Step 8. Participants respond to these concerns by improving upon the ideas they have previously produced. Again, the ideas are all recorded.

Step 9. The client is invited by the leader to say whether he sees what he regards as a possible solution. (If not, then he is invited to select another statement for exploration, back to Step 5 in fact—and if necessary the workshop can loop between Steps 5 and 9 for some time). If a client believes there is a possible solution, he is asked to explain what it is in his own words. They are recorded verbatim.

Step 10. The leader checks that the client believes the possible solution to be feasible and asks the client to say what his next steps will be towards implementation. The "next steps" are recorded.

These examples should serve to show that plans are detailed, predetermined, and action-orientated. These characteristics distinguish them from vaguer things called intentions. As remarked earlier, intentions have a poor track record when measured in terms of their actual translation into action. We all know what happens to New Year resolutions! Resolve is not enough; we have to plan. The difference between a plan and an intention is only of degree, not of kind. The difference is really one of specificity. Our New Year resolutions are vague. They only state *what* we want to do and never give sufficient attention to *how* we shall manage it. A plan devotes much more time to spelling out how something shall be accomplished.

This emphasis on planning rather than intending is

not new. There are plenty of examples of people putting plans into action in all sorts of small ways in everyday life. Do you ever tie a knot in your handkerchief to help ensure that you will remember something? If so, that is an example of planning to remember rather than just intending to remember. Of course, the plan might not work but its existence certainly pushes up the probability of success. Do you ever compile daily or weekly "to do" lists for yourself? If so, that again is an example of a simple behavior plan. Have you ever written notes to yourself and left them propped up somewhere obvious—on the telephone, on a mantlepiece? "Counting sheep" is a plan some people adopt to get them to sleep quickly. "Counting to 10" before you speak is a plan some people use to make it more likely that they will engage their brain before opening their mouth. I once knew a manager who decided that he talked too much and didn't listen hard enough. So, on certain selected occasions (*which* occasions was part of his plan), he put a bit of masking tape over his mouth. His plan was so effective in changing his behavior that it was not long before he could dispense with the tape completely! In all these cases, notice that the hallmark of a plan is its attention to detail, its specificity. Yet it is this very characteristic that often irritates people. They will complain of "hair splitting" or of "using a sledge hammer to crack a nut." Changing behavior isn't just a nut: It is a remarkable accomplishment and one which this book should help you to achieve.

BASIC STEPS INVOLVED
IN CHANGING BEHAVIOR

In a sense, we are all in the behavior change business. The essence of interacting, when there are objectives to be achieved in face to face interactions, is to use your own behavior to influence that of others. In these circumstances, behavior change, or some people prefer the word "modification" since it does not sound so drastic, is involved in two ways. First, there is your ability to control your own behavior in accordance with the objectives. This is, if you like, self-change. As we have already seen, changes you make to your behavior will bring about observable changes in other people's because of the effects of behavior "shaping." However, sometimes we want to change someone else's behavior by working out a behavior plan *together with them*. This is exactly what appraisal sessions are supposed to do, for example. In effect, we are a third party trying to encourage and help someone else to embark on self-change.

The basic ingredients for change remain the same, whether we are concerned with modifying our own behavior consciously and deliberately, or with getting another person to modify theirs. In both cases, the ingredients for behavior modification seem to be:

   a. The need to observe behavior (our own and/or other people's) with some precision, leading to an awareness of what changes are necessary
   b. The need to plan, again with some precision, how the behavior will be changed
   c. The need to stick to the plan by monitoring it and having feedback about its effects.

Behavior modification programs in schools, hospitals, and prisons are based on these simple principles, and we need to ensure that they are embodied in our own less lavish plans.

Let us exemplify these principles by tracing them through a simple "everyday" example. What about that maddening habit so many people seem to have of saying "you know" at frequent intervals! Let us assume that someone else is displaying this behavior and that we want to change it.

The first step is to *notice* the behavior, to have observed it. Earlier, we established that all behavior is always overt and can therefore be seen and/or heard. I argued that this was an important characteristic of interactive behavior and distinguished it clearly from, for example, underlying feelings and emotions. We can only draw inferences about them, or a less polite way of putting it is that we can only guess about the presence or otherwise of invisible things like feelings, motives, and intelligence. We only have access to them via the observation of behavior itself. So we can observe that "you know" behavior in a "straightforward" manner.

The second point is less obvious and rather complicated; it harks back to something discussed in Chapter 1.

It is that we do not merely observe other people's behavior (or anything else, for that matter) in a dispassionate, utterly accurate way: We add and subtract bits in rather an interesting manner. We use our senses (sight, hearing, smell, touch, and so on) to assemble data about our surrounding environment. We do not take it all in because there is too much of it. So we select, paying close attention to some data, only taking cursory notice of other aspects, and taking no notice at all of the remainder. The complication, however, concerns the way in which we process what data does come in. This is usually referred to as the perceptual process. Perceiving is not the same as seeing or hearing because the observer is active in *organizing* incoming information. We have to interpret this information, giving it meaning, slotting it against a whole store of accumulated previous experiences, checking it against our likes and dislikes. By the time we have finished, the perceptual process may have markedly distorted whatever was originally picked up by our senses. Our senses are neutral—they do not judge or assess; they just transmit as swiftly and accurately as their physiological state permits. Our perceptual processes do the rest.

There are many dramatic examples of this. We may *see* clouds in the sky but *perceive* faces or other meaningful shapes. We may see an ink blot but perceive a butterfly. We may see a laborer leaning on his shovel but perceive a lazy Irishman. We may hear someone say "You know" at frequent intervals and perceive a pathetic person who has a limited vocabulary, or a person who is unduly anxious, or a person who clearly hasn't much intelligence, or a person who comes from a working class background, or. . .well, take your pick!

The implications of this difference between the observation of behavior and its perception are considerable. For example, it is easy to confuse our perceptual understanding of a piece of behavior with an explanation about the causes for the behavior. We can soon come to believe that whenever someone says "You know," it is *caused* by some emotional state—anxiety, we might conclude. But notice that while it might be easy for us to believe that this is the cause, at best it is a theory—or a guess—or a convenient way of reducing the options and making us feel that we understand why people behave as they do. Most of us have built up a whole set of beliefs or assumptions against which we can slot observed behaviors with the minimum of fuss.

Another implication is that our perceptions of behavior usually scan people themselves for explanations rather than the characteristics of different situations with which people are faced. In other words, we try to explain behavior by attributing motives, emotions, and underlying causes to people. We move rapidly from the *observation* that Joe gets through less work than Bill to conclude that Joe is lazy. From then on, Joe is perceived as being in possession of a quality known as laziness. And yet, of course, Joe isn't always lazy. Sometimes he behaves in ways which, despite our biased perception of him, we would have to conclude were far from amounting to laziness: doing his part, for example, washing the car on a Sunday morning, playing with his children, collecting stamps.

So it can't be Joe who is lazy. It must be Joe in *certain situations* who is lazy. This means that, if anything, it is the influence of external factors in the various situations which Joe encounters that is more likely to hold the key to understanding his behavior rather than things we might infer about Joe himself. This is a vital point because, as we have seen, when we interact with someone *we* are an important aspect of *their* external environment. Thus we are able, through our behavior, to have a considerable *causal* influence on their behavior.

We can check this thinking out by returning to the example of the person who says "You know" at frequent intervals. Clearly, our observation of the frequent occurrence of this piece of behavior is a basic prerequisite before we can set about working out how to change it. Having a theory about *why* this behavior is indulged in does not seem to be a basic prerequisite. As we have seen, it might be anxiety, it might be the effects of a limited vocabulary—it might be a whole host of things. So we need to steer clear of perceiving this behavior in that sort of way. It is enough that we perceive it as a distraction: in other words, that we find ourselves noticing the "You knows" to such an extent that doing so ties up too many of our observational resources and we do not absorb the content of what he is saying to us; or that we perceive it as something which irritates us, which we do not like.

How can we change it, having noticed it? Clearly, it is not enough to say "I wish you'd stop saying 'You know' all the time," or to say "You say 'You know' so often that I'm finding it a real distraction. Couldn't you cut it out?" There's clearly more to getting people to change their behavior— even in the case of this simple example—than simply telling them to do so. This is why "nagging" is such an uneconomic strategy for influencing change in the required direction. Wives must learn to plan if they really want to change their husband's behavior!

What, then, do we need to do to influence someone to change the verbal "You know" habit? We saw earlier that the basic steps involved observing the behavior, planning how to change it, and sticking to the plan. One approach would be to think of a way in which we can change *our* behavior as an antidote to the other person's" You know" habit. Behavior shaping rears its head again. We might, for example, plan to interrupt them before they can include an unnecessary "You know" to the end of what they are saying. Alternatively, we might try avoiding the use of open-ended questions, where we are able to exercise less control over the answer, and stick to a series of specific closed questions. This might be quite dramatic in cutting, or even abolishing, the "You know" rate in the other person.

What, though, if we want to help the other person to help themselves in changing their behavior? We only need one extra step. Instead of merely observing the behavior ourselves, we shall need to share our observations with the other person. This is known as "feedback." Feeding back involves us in finding some way of getting the other person to be as aware of the selected aspect of his behavior as we are. It may be enough simply to tell them about it, or it might be more appropriate to lead them, via questioning, to see it for themselves. So now the steps leading to behavior change are:·

Step 1. We must observe the behavior.

Step 2. We must feed back our observations so that the other person is as aware of the behavioral characteristic as we are.

Step 3. We must help them to plan precisely how they are going to change.

Step 4. We must leave them to stick to the plan (unless we can become an integral part of the plan itself, in which case we must stick to our bit of it too).

How might these steps be accomplished in our "You know" example? The word "might" should be emphasized here. There may be many alternative ways of going about it which would be equally successful. What follows is not *the* prescription for reducing or abolishing "You know" behavior in our colleagues; it is simply an example of a possible way.

Step 1: Observing

Monitor conversation they are having with someone else by simply counting the number of times they say "You know" for a timed period. Then calculate what the "You know" rate is per minute.

Step 2: Feeding Back

Then say something like: "I hope you don't mind my saying so, but I could not help noticing how many times you said 'You know' during that conversation. I reckon that on the average, it comes out at roughly six 'You knows' per minute."

Let them be suitably shocked.

Say, "Do you want to cut this rate?"

Let them say whatever they want to say.

Say, "What impression do you think saying 'You know' every ten seconds has on other people?"

Let them say whatever they want to say.

Say, "What would be a reasonable 'You know' rate, in your opinion?" Let them give you a target figure.

Step 3: Planning

Say, "Fine. Now, how are you going to get it down to that?"

Let them come up with something.

Say, "But have you any ideas on what you can actually *do* in the future to ensure success?"

Gradually build up a plan that they can adhere to in reducing the "You know" count to the target. The actual plan will vary from person to person, but here is an example.

On Mondays, Wednesdays, and Fridays carry a small note book in your pocket with "YOU KNOW" written in large letters on page one. Every time you interact, get the notebook out and have it open in front of you. Whenever you catch yourself saying "You know," put a tally mark on the page. You can soon dispense with the notebook because there aren't any "You knows" to record!

This example of changing someone's behavior has been deliberately simple in order to illustrate the basic steps involved. A recent article by a behavior therapist outlined the behavioral approach to losing weight. The principles were exactly the same. Painstaking attention to the behavior of eating leading to a detailed, tailor-made behavior plan. Just to demonstrate the similarity with behavior plans already cited in this chapter, here is part of the weight watcher's behavior plan quoted from a recent magazine article.

> Where meals are concerned, it is essential that casual eating be eliminated by making oneself think about eating as a separate piece of behavior not linked to anything else. Eating from one corner of a cluttered table or from a tray must be stopped. The whole table must be used, and this must be cleared of everything apart from the place setting, glass, pepper, salt, and so on. During the meal, the dieter's full concentration must be on the food. Books, magazines, and television, as distractions from eating, are out. The food should be served as attractively as possible, especially if there is a reduction in helping size as part of the program. It can be helpful to serve smaller helpings on a smaller plate, as this tends to disguise the reduction of actual intake.
>
> During the meal, the subject is encouraged to think about the taste and the texture of the food and told to put down the knife and fork between each mouthful. If eating in company, he should also make conversation between mouthfuls. Before taking a drink, he must ensure that his mouth is empty of food. After the meal, left-over food should be thrown straight into the garbage can to eliminate the temptation of finishing it while clearing up. All these activities help to break previously established eating patterns. After such a piece of appropriate behavior has been carried out, the subject is told to reward himself immediately by doing something pleasant from a previously agreed list of "positive reinforcements." It is essential that whatever reward has been chosen—going for a walk, making a phone call, or having a cigarette—is done immediately upon completion of the behavior.

PLANNING BEHAVIOR IN THE LIGHT
OF OBJECTIVES

It is time to link behavior plans, be they for ourselves or for other people, to objectives. To return to the theme launched in Chapter 2 that coupled situations, objectives, and behavior together into a unified system: This can best be done by returning to the example given in Chapter 2 on pages 31–32. The end-of-interaction objective (page 31) and the behavior plan (page 32) were described in advance of subsequent chapters that explored objectives and behavior more thoroughly. Perhaps you can now see how it is possible to tighten up the behavior plan by using the language of the behavior categories. It is almost as though we need to dot the I's and cross the T's of the plan by working out which specific bits of behavior we must cling to in safeguarding the objectives and putting the plan into action. Planning can be envisaged at two levels: strategic and tactical. Strategies are couched in much more general terms than tactics. In this sense, the behavior plan on pages 31–32 is strategic. It only hints at the precise behavior categories that are vital to its implementation.

What, then, would the tactical part of the plan be? And how necessary is it?

In that particular case, bearing in mind both the objective and the strategy, I feel the tactics should be:

> The behavior I will use most is seeking suggestions/
> proposals. When I have to—and certainly only half as
> much as I seek them—I'll make suggestions myself
> and/or build. I will also support, and, when checking
> that I have recorded an idea correctly, seek clarification.
> I forbid myself to propose, disagree, or difficulty state
> on this occasion.

It is by consciously arranging my behavior at this tactical level of specificity that I simultaneously ensure that my behaviors are in step with my objective, and that I discipline myself to implement the behavior plan. This is why I claimed earlier that a detailed plan was the "secret."

How necessary is the tactical level? Let me put it this way: In the unlikely event of someone saying that I couldn't have both strategy and tactics as part of the behavior plan, and that one of them had to go, I would retain tactics. I have found it entirely possible to commit myself to objectives and tactics, and within those constraints to give myself room for maneuvering and for flexibility when it came to the strategy. You can test the feasibility of this to some extent by looking back at the objective on page 31 and seeing whether the main tactics just listed are obvious at that stage without referring to the strategy. Surely they are. References in the objective to "encouraging them to come up with lots of ideas and suggestions," "each has produced at least three suggestions" scream out for seeking suggestions as a priority behavior. The standard about spontaneous comments on the rewarding/involving atmosphere of the meeting argues for behaviors like supporting and building and warns against proposing, disagreeing, and difficulty stating. Understanding what is involved in setting an adequate objective, the shaping effects of different behaviors, and the the need to plan is enough.

In summary, I use behavior categories quite literally as a guarantee that my behavior plan will be sufficiently detailed to be actionable. It just so happens that the very same language, that of behavior categories, is also being used to monitor, unobtrusively but consciously, the behaviors as they happen. This means that the monitoring gives instant feedback about my ability to stick to the plan and its ability to shape the behavior of others in the direction required by the objectives. In this way, the plan and the monitoring become mutually reinforcing.

What if the predetermined plan proves inappropriate? Suppose it is based on certain assumptions about the way someone will be behaving, and, in the event, that these are false? If you discover that the tactics you had singled out for yourself are entirely inappropriate, that is an indication that you failed to think them through adequately in relation to the objective. When this happens, you should hurriedly arrive at some fresh tactics that are more contaminated by the objective than the abandoned ones were. It is much more likely that you will find your tactics redundant rather than in need of drastic revision. This frequently happens if you *assumed* that you were going to be up against it in trying to persuade someone to adopt a course of action and accordingly would arm yourself with lots of shaping behaviors. If, once the interaction starts, you find your fears were unfounded, it is merely a question of toning down your use of shapers. The need to make on-the-spot adjustments of this kind reinforces the importance of continuous monitoring of behavior and conscious control so that it remains in step with objectives. It also argues for a strategy that will not straitjacket us. Hence the emphasis on objectives and tactics. In the end, where you.put the emphasis in your behavior plan—on strategy, or tactics, or both—is a matter of personal taste. I admit to favoring tactics. Many people, however, find working through the strategy invaluable as a means of bridging the gap between where objectives leave off and tactics begin. Also, many people use the preparation of a strategy as a means of deciding on their objective. This may seem like putting the cart before the horse, but a trade-off between objective and strategy can work well so long as you avoid the temptation of thinking that a strategy is an adequate replacement for an objective. Chapter 4 was at pains to distinguish between activities or plans on the one hand and objectives on the other. If this distinction is becoming hazy, it would be worth checking back through the first half of Chapter 4.

EXERCISES IN PRODUCING
BEHAVIOR PLANS
FOR FACE TO FACE ENCOUNTERS

Chapter 4 provided six situations as part of an exercise in setting realistic objectives. We can now use those same situations and the earlier work we did on thinking out objectives as our background data for generating strategy and tactics.

Each situation, together with its objective, is repeated here to save you checking back, so that you can work out, preferably on a bit of scrap paper, what you consider to be an in step behavior plan, including both strategy and tactics. Immediately after the chapter summary, I have set out my "solutions"; once again, it is important to accept that they are not offered as the "right" answers. They are merely a basis for comparison between the plans that I think appropriate and your own work. Your strategy, in particular, could vary considerably and still be entirely actionable and successful in maximizing the achievement of the objective. Really wide divergence on the behavior tactics is less likely, however. If, for example, I have planned to abstain from certain behaviors and you have elected to use them as those most appropriate to the objective, that is cause for concern. Especially since, for the purpose of this exercise, we are sharing an identical starting point in the objectives. Armed with the same objectives, our tactics at least should be substantially similar.

Here are the situations, together with their respective objectives. My thoughts on behavior plans appear immediately before the chapter summary on pages 193 to 198.

Situation 1: Delegation Problem

One of your subordinates has one real shortcoming: He will not delegate. Whenever there is any semblance of a crisis, he goes in and does the job himself. When tackled on this, he claims that his people respect him for being able to do a better job than they can or says that he likes "to keep his hand in." You suspect that his people resent these interventions whenever something is getting really interesting and regard them as a vote of no confidence in their work. Furthermore, you have noticed that this inability or unwillingness to delegate results in your subordinate taking too much on himself. He frequently stays late to "catch up" and increasingly fails to get jobs done by their deadlines. You decide that you have got to tackle this problem and get him to delegate more.

> *Objective for Situation 1:*
> To have produced a plan with X which sorts out which of the jobs he is currently doing himself can be given to someone else and identifies that someone. The plan will also include what he can do to stop intervening in a crisis.
> I shall have been successful if:
> a. The plan we have produced includes details on what, how, who, where, and when.
> b. The plan has allocated a minimum of four jobs which X is currently doing himself to someone else.
> c. X has subscribed to the plan and said that it has been a helpful session; also that he is going to put the plan into action.
> d. X has himself suggested that sometime in the future there should be a further meeting to review the success of the plan and to make another one if necessary.
> e. This has been achieved within two hours.

Situation 2: Procrastinating Boss

Your boss is a renowned verbal rambler and procrastinator. You need a decision—urgently.

In 30 minutes, a very good customer prospect is due to arrive to meet you. You have already had a series of meetings and things are looking good. Three days ago, you had a session with your boss when you asked if you might make some concession to this prospective customer which you are sure will clinch the deal. You didn't bother him with precise details of the concessions you expect are necessary; you were more interested in getting his blessing in principle, with some guidance about how much room for maneuvering you were permitted.

You have already pushed him twice since then for a decision. Once he said he was still thinking about it, and the second time he was just rushing off to some meeting or other. You are now going to see him to try to get a decision; you predict that he will not have made his mind up and will still be "worrying" about it.

Objective for Situation 2:
To have got him to agree to all the concessions I am likely to need within 20 minutes.
I shall have been successful if I achieve this in such a way that:

a. He will have shown no sign of resentment at being "nagged" or pushed into a decision.

b. He will have shared the contribution rate with me to a maximum of 50 per cent.

c. He will have said that he is quite happy with the concession arrangement.

Situation 3: Taking Over New Departments

You have just been appointed departmental manager of a newly formed department. Your department contains three branches. One of them you know intimately, having run it yourself for three years. It is now run by one of the people in that branch with whom you worked closely and successfully. The two other branches are a service branch which you never used or thought much of before, and a branch selling a fairly technical product direct to the customer. You are not familiar with either the product or with operating in a direct-to-the-customer environment.

The branch from which you came is in many ways more advanced in its work than the other two. Its staff are on average higher paid, for instance, and its "specialness" has been known to cause resentment.

You only know the two branch managers to say "hello" to and you are anxious to get off to a good start with them both. So you have arranged to meet them, one at a time, for an initial "getting to know each other" couple of hours.

> *Objective for Situation 3:*
> (For both branch managers in turn.) To have produced a list of items for our next working meeting together.
> I shall have been successful if:
> a. The list has at least six items on it, all of which genuinely require both of us.
> b. It has been produced in not less than one and not more than two hours.
> c. He has contributed a minimum of half the items listed himself.
> d. The date and time for the next meeting will have been agreed upon between us before we break up.
> e. He has said that he looks forward to the next meeting in such a way that I'm inclined to think he really means it.

Situation 4: The Ideas Man

You have a colleague with whom you have worked on a number of projects in the past. You know him as a guy who is always coming up with ideas, some good, some mediocre, and some appalling. He seems to go for quantity of ideas and to let other people worry about quality. This has not earned him a very good reputation, since the work "culture" seems to put a higher premium on good ideas rather than a lot of ideas.

He has sent you a draft of a new idea he has had, worked out in enormous detail. He wants to come and discuss it with you as someone whose views are important to him, not as someone who will be involved in any future implementation of the idea. Unfortunately, you think the idea is completely unworkable in its present form, although you recognize there is a germ of value in it.

He respects your opinion. You hope to steer him away from making a fool of himself without losing his respect.

Objective for Situation 4:
To have got him to agree to a substantial rethinking of his idea in order to make it workable.
I shall have been successful if:

a. He has accepted that at least half of the difficulties I raise in relation to his idea *are* genuine snags.

b. He has said in his own words without any prompting from me, that he now sees that the "culture" is geared to appreciate the quality as well as the quantity of ideas.

c. He has told me that I've done him a big favor and asked if he might return at some later stage to check out the modified ideas with me.

d. This has been achieved in a maximum of one hour.

Situation 5: Activity Diaries

You have to brief a group of your subordinates on the part they are to play in a nationwide exercise to obtain information about how they spend their working time. It involves them in keeping an activity diary each day for a month: a laborious and unrewarding task.

You are experiencing some irritation, as it is not long since a similar request was made. No one, including you, heard the outcome of the previous study, and several doubted its necessity.

You have put it on the agenda of a meeting you are due to have with all your subordinates, and you wonder how you can break the news of this imposed chore and get enough commitment from them at the same time.

Objective for Situation 5:
To have got them to identify the benefits *to us* of keeping

activity diaries and to have planned how to cash in on some of those benefits.

I shall have been successful if:

a. A minimum of half my subordinates have said that they agree that the benefits we have identified *are real* benefits.

b. Our plans do not cut across or interfere with the data head office needs from the activity records.

c. The plan we have produced includes the usual elements of how, who, where, and when.

d. Our plan will not be so ambitious that putting it into effect is likely to interfere with work, other than the normal interruption caused by keeping an activity record accurately for one month.

e. I have judged that the plan, when put into action, will succeed in achieving 50 per cent of the identified benefits.

f. This has been achieved in a maximum of two hours.

Situation 6: Salesman's Expenses

You are an area sales manager appointed just six months ago. One of your best salesmen, with an extremely good record, is inclined to "pad" quite a lot of his expenses. He is on a basic salary plus bonus system, and his earnings are substantial. You were shocked by the level of these expenses from the very start, but approved the claim for the first two months without questioning anything with him. You knew this was sheer cowardice at the time, but hoped the situation would resolve itself. It didn't, and so in the third month you spoke to him about the high level of his expenses. He was sullen but agreed to watch them. Since then, you haven't been able to detect the slightest change.

You are about to meet him to take up the matter of expenses for the second time. You expect him to feel that his good sales record more than justifies the level of expenses, and to see you as being unnecessarily petty in raising the matter again.

Objective for Situation 6:
To have got him to set a new standard of performance for himself which controls his level of expenses.
I shall have been successful if:

a. He has set the standard, not me.

b. The standard he has set accords with my own ideas on a suitable level of expenses.

c. He has agreed that the standard will be binding for the next three months, after which we will review it.

d. He has said that he now sees that a "good" salesman is not just someone who brings in sales, but someone who has a feel for his revenue to cost ratio.

e. This has been achieved within a maximum of one and a half hours.

BEHAVIOR PLAN FOR SITUATION 1

Strategy

My overall strategy is to get X to see the need for a plan which tackles his reluctance to delegate. I want him to feel that the work we do together in producing the plan is worthwhile so that he produces lots of ideas himself and doesn't just acquiesce.

So I'll start by asking him lots of questions about how things are going and gradually "close in" on issues to do with him being too busy. Having got him to agree that he *is* too busy, I'll start wondering, in an off-the-top-of-my-head way, about whether something could be done about it. This way, I'll slip in my idea about actually drawing up a plan which he could cling to for a while as a discipline in getting over his problem.

I'll try to get *him* to think of items for inclusion in the plan, and only put forward my own ideas if he doesn't come up with them or with ideas which are every bit as good as mine.

Tactics

Top behaviors on my part are seeking suggestions/proposals and suggesting.

Second string behaviors from me are seeking clarification (particularly in the early stages of the interaction) and building.

BEHAVIOR PLAN FOR SITUATION 2

Strategy

I'll work out in precise detail all the concessions I am likely to need *in advance* of the meeting. This is in contrast to what I did three days ago. My idea is to be as positive and as specific as I possibly can. This is to reduce the likelihood of further doubts and procrastinations from him.

I'll have to take a risk during this short interaction by referring to the prospective sale as if it has already happened and is a dead certainty.

I'll be absolutely straight with him about my objectives and the concessions I'm likely to need—not asking for anything more or less. It would not help to "negotiate" by pitching my request higher than it need be because (a) since he is a procrastinator he won't be able to respond to this sort of treatment and won't be able to say "no" and thus prune my request down to size; (b) I haven't the time.

I will avoid peppering my remarks with little comforters such as "Of course, I mightn't need to go that far," since to do so will give the impression that things aren't cut and dried (and that will be like a red rag to a procrastinator).

I'm going to say everything at a comprehensible, but punchy, pace.

Tactics

I'll confine my behavior to two categories only: proposing (top behavior by far) and seeking clarification.

The other categories are *out*—especially seeking suggestions, suggesting and building.

BEHAVOR PLAN FOR SITUATION 3

Strategy

To cut all social niceties and references to the past to an acceptable minimum. To start the "real" working interaction going as soon as possible, as a means of reducing any embarrassment and of getting the interactive flow going.

I'll start by saying that I'd like the meeting to be useful to us both, and has he any ideas on how we might structure it so that it is? I'll listen to what he suggests and compare it (inwardly) with the objectives I'm after. If it isn't close enough to what I want, then I'll suggest mine in an involving way.

I'll spend up to 50 per cent of the available time for the meeting on coordinating the meeting's and our objectives, because this is hard work which we can both get stuck into very quickly indeed.

Once our objectives are agreed upon, I'll do more "sitting back" and let him come up with most of the items for the list.

Tactics

Top behaviors: seeking suggestion, suggesting, and seeking clarification. Next: building and supporting.

BEHAVIOR PLAN FOR SITUATION 4

Strategy

In advance of arranging to see him, I'll list every difficulty I can think of in relation to his idea. I will then

settle on, say, eight which, if they are to be overcome, will
need the idea to be completely rethought.

I'll telephone him to fix the meeting, and warn him
that I can see lots of difficulties so maybe I'm not going to be
much use to him? This should help to ensure that he comes
expecting difficulties rather than enthusiasm.

When we meet, I'll ask him what he would like me
to do, and work him round to agreeing that I should play
"devil's advocate." Before beginning that role, I will tell him
that the difficulties I'm going to concentrate on getting his
agreement to were short-listed from a longer list. And I'll tell
him what criterion I used in arriving at it (that these difficulties indicate a substantial re-think of the whole idea rather
than a bit of tinkering here and there).

Then I'll play "devil's advocate," according to plan.

Tactics

Top behaviors, almost to the total exclusion of all
others; difficulty stating, disagreeing, and seeking clarification; also, some seeking suggestions.

BEHAVIOR PLAN FOR SITUATION 5

Strategy

Since we are lumbered with this chore anyway, and,
since we didn't get anything out of it last time, I'm out to
make sure that we do it for *us* this time, and comply with the
head office request at the same time.

I'll start by "coming clean" and tell them about the
dictum. I will not grumble or refer to "them" but just be
matter of fact about it.

I'll then say: ". . .So, since we have got to do this
anyway and since it involves us all in a lot of effort—as we
know from last time—I wondered if it might be an idea to
work out how we ourselves can benefit from all this. Can

anyone think of what *we* could get out of it?" I will list the points as they come up on a big flipchart pad or blackboard which everyone can see. I will be careful to hold back from making suggestions myself. In fact, I will only make a suggestion if (a) there aren't any coming from them at all, and (b) if I can slip it in among lots of others without them noticing it came from me.

When there aren't any more ideas on benefits, I'll suggest that we see which of them we can hope to achieve by working out a plan of action. I'll kick the process off by giving them the four standards I have previously set to do with the plan (my way of keeping control over the planning without actually having to shoot them down all the time). They can then work out the plan. I'll put my oar in as necessary, but I'd rather they imposed this plan on me rather than the other way round.

Tactics

Top behaviors: seeking suggestions and seeking clarification. Back up—suggesting and building. I will be a low contributor.

BEHAVIOR PLAN FOR SITUATION 6

Strategy

I'll start by telling him that I have been remiss in letting things slide and that I have been consistently shocked at the level of his expenses, even taking into account his excellent sales record.

I'll show him some calculations I'll have prepared expressing his expenses as a percentage of the revenue he brings in and contrast it with the percentages characteristic of his colleagues.

I'll challenge him to reduce his percentage by never talking about whether he *wants* to do it (I'll assume he doesn't), and concentrate on asking him whether he can do it. Can he still turn in the highest revenue of all the salesmen and have the lowest percentage on expenses?

I'll tell him that I would like to agree on a standard with him and counsel him to be realistic since standards, once set, are apt to become a depressing liability if they are unobtainable. I'll ask him what that standard should be.

I'll help him in any way I can in the setting of the standard, other than set it for him.

Tactics

Top behaviors: proposing and suggesting (in that order). Second string: seeking suggestions.

SUMMARY

The chapter has attempted to round off its predecessors by concentrating on the mechanics of planning behavior. Behavior planning was hailed as the means of ensuring that behavior is changed and modified in the desired way.

A plan, whether it be pieced together considerably or fractionally in advance of implementation, was defined as a detailed expression of a predetermined course of action. A plan is concerned with spelling out *how* something is going to be done, and this distinguishes it from an intention which stops short of *how* and merely states *what*. A number of examples of different behavior plans were given to point up their attention to detail.

The chapter then went on to look more closely at the steps involved in changing both our own and someone else's behavior. We saw that observation, planning, monitoring, and feedback were essential ingredients, whether the plan was concerned with the modification of relatively "simple" pieces of behavior or more complex behavioral habits.

Finally, the chapter showed how the language of the behavior categories can double as a shorthand when putting together a behavior plan, particularly at a detailed, tactical level. The suggestion was made that objectives and tactics, provided they are precise and unambiguous enough, can "take the strain," leaving the strategic elements of the plan more adaptable. The final conclusion was that the interplay between objective, strategy, and tactics was largely a matter of personal taste, provided corners were not cut on objectives and tactics, the two most specific areas, in particular.

The chapter concluded with a series of behavior planning exercises.

9

What Is Interactive Competence?

This is going to be a foolhardy chapter! It will spell out, in precise behavioral terms, the main hallmarks of an interactively skilled person in the hope that this will prove a useful distillation of points made in previous chapters.

I describe this venture as foolhardy because it would be so much easier to dodge this level of explicitness and thus avoid leaving myself open to protests like:

> "The listing of behaviors typical of an interactively skilled person reduced it all to a mechanistic level and completely missed essential characteristics like human warmth and understanding."

> "Interactive competence cannot be defined: It is something you recognize when you see it but it can't be defined in cold print."

> "If that is interactive skill—count me out!"

But not being completely explicit and not pinpointing what is involved in being interactively skillful, in *behavioral terms*, would be an obvious piece of hypocrisy on my part. So, risky though it is, I am going to conclude by doing it.

The main risk is the old one, encountered many times throughout this text, of failing to relate the various hallmarks to specific sets of circumstances and objectives. Clearly, some of the hallmarks will be applicable sometimes and positively not applicable at other times. The hallmarks that follow are not, therefore, panacea-like "golden" rules.

The hallmarks are divided into two sections. First come 20 attributes that you can observe *at the time*, while in interaction with a skillful person. This is followed by five extra things that you could observe *over time*, or over a series of interactions. In neither list are the hallmarks set down in any order of importance.

HALLMARKS OF AN INTERACTIVELY SKILLED PERSON THAT CAN BE OBSERVED DURING AN INTERACTION

a. He explicitly states his understanding of the objectives for the interaction and invites others present to do the same. If understandings differ, he either seeks out a compromise set of objectives that are mutually satisfactory or suggests a strategy that ensures both (or more) sets of objectives are substantially achieved. He never fobs off difficulties in matching objectives by assuming that they overlap sufficiently when they do not or by saying: "We all know what we mean."

b. If the appropriateness of his objective is challenged, he can justify it in relation to the situation and show that it is realistic and yet challenging.

c. He keeps his behavior in step with the objectives of the interaction and does not wander off down irrelevant side tracks.

d. He explicitly labels his own behavior whenever he considers it likely to aid its reception (which is quite often).

e. He seeks behavioral clarification whenever he is not clear how to interpret the behavior of others.

f. He often makes overt comments on his own behavior in relation to that of others, thus showing that he is conscious of it and concerned about its effects.

g. He keeps his verbal and nonverbal behaviors in perfect accord with one another.

h. He conducts himself in such a way that you, as an observer of his behavior, believe him to be genuine and are not suspicious of hidden ulterior motives, double dealing, and the like. Even if he does not say what his objectives are, you can piece them together accurately from his behavior.

i. He behaves in such a way that you, on the receiving end of his behavior, feel rewarded by the encounter. He does this in a variety of ways—by using your name, for example, by looking at you sufficiently, by laughing at your jokes, by showing that he has heard what you said, by expressing feelings and not just transmitting facts, and by supporting or building on your ideas more often than he rejects them.

j. He "freewheels" behind others' behavior only when he has established that, in so doing, the objectives are being achieved adequately. In these circumstances, he does not push himself to maintain control of the conversation or seek to be behaviorally the most powerful or the most "noisy."

k.. He explicitly announces mini behavior plans (such as "I've been thinking about this and thought it best if I outlined my view of the problem first, then explored how yours differ before trying to think of solutions together").

l. He never produces a string of different behaviors without summarizing so that others are clear which bit(s) to react to.

m. He never acquiesces silently (because he knows that silence is a behavior it is infuriatingly difficult for others to interpret).

n. He produces explicit suggestions and proposals that contain a possible course of action rather than an implied one.

o. He never gets into a disagreement spiral.

p. In problem solving/decision making/conflict resolving interactions, he rations his "other behavior" (seeking and giving information, reiterating and giving clarification) to a maximum of half of all the behaviors he produces.

q. When seeking clarification, he does so by testing his understanding (i.e., saying what he has understood and asking to be "corrected") more often than in any other way.

r. He pushes for the agreement of specific action plans rather than being content with intentions.

s. When criticizing someone, he is always constructive in the sense that he produces a suggestion along with every criticism.

t. When in the wrong or inadequate in some way he admits it rather than pretend that he is right or adequate.

HALLMARKS OF AN INTERACTIVELY SKILLED PERSON THAT CAN BE OBSERVED OVER A NUMBER OF INTERACTIONS

a. He is successful in achieving his objectives, either totally, so that there is no discrepancy between the predicted and the actual outcome, or nearly totally, with only little bits of slippage here and there.

b. He makes significant modifications to his behavior, sometimes predominantly seeking, sometimes giving, sometimes reacting, and so on.

c. He consciously arranges his behavior whenever he is aware of wishing to achieve an objective, wishes to impress and/or influence, is in a conflict situation where objectives clash, is in a delicate situation where emotions run high, and, finally, where any of the above apply *and* he is confined to a short face to face interaction.

d. He always does what he says he will do (his actions do *not* speak any louder than his words).

e. He learns from his interactive experiences by explicitly reviewing his performance in the light of his objectives and his plan and makes regular references to lessons he has learned and behavior insights he has had.

Just for good measure, a final hallmark could be that an interactively skilled person unhesitatingly agrees that the above criteria *do* encapsulate all that is distinctive about an interactively competent person! Even if this was not so, interactively skilled people would want to add to the list rather than reject items. I have certainly found that the interactively skilled are good at articulating criteria of the kind listed. This is not surprising, since one of the consistent themes running through our scrutiny of interactive skills has been doing things consciously rather than unconsciously or unthinkingly. The correlation between behaving consciously and being able to describe the process is very high. Accordingly, I am sceptical about considering someone interactively accomplished if they are unable to articulate how they do it. I am even more sceptical about considering someone interactively competent just because they can talk about the process. If the proof of the pudding is in the eating, the proof of interactive competence is in the interacting.